THE CURSE OF
SHERLOCK HOLMES

T0096691

THE CURSE OF SHERLOCK HOLMES

The BASIL RATHBONE Story

by David CLAYTON

The History Press

First published 2020
This paperback edition published 2021

The History Press
97 St George's Place, Cheltenham,
Gloucestershire, GL50 3QB
www.thehistorypress.co.uk

British Library Cataloguing in Publication Data.
A catalogue record for this book is available from the British Library.

ISBN 978 0 7509 9747 8

Typesetting and origination by The History Press
Printed and bound in Great Britain by TJ Books Limited, Padstow, Cornwall.

Trees for Life

For Mum. My biggest fan.
And for Marcia. Basil's biggest fan.

Contents

Acknowledgements

Within, walls continued upright, bricks met neatly, floors were
firm, and doors were sensibly shut; silence lay steadily against
the wood and stone of Hill House, and whatever walked there,
walked alone.

Shirley Jackson, *The Haunting of Hill House*

The above is one of my favourite lines in all of literature. But what
has it got to do with Basil Rathbone? Nothing. It does, however, have
something to do with the writing of this book, which was also put
together brick by brick (or word by word) with the floors (hopefully)
firm and the doors (occasionally) shut.

Silence did indeed lay steadily at some points – several years, in
fact – but at no stage did I walk alone.

In simple terms, this book would have been incredibly difficult
to write but for the fantastic work of Marcia Jessen and Neve
Rendell, both huge fans of Basil Rathbone and dedicated sleuths
that Sir Arthur Conan Doyle himself would have been proud of.
Marcia and Neve allowed me to mine their considerable collection
of Rathbone material in the hope that I would be the biographer

who would write about not only Basil's life in the theatre and the movies, but his life and times away from the public eye – and certainly not focus solely on his time as Sherlock Holmes.

Marcia, I have to say, has gone above and beyond. No query was too great and her permission to share the mountains of research was generous and selfless. I owe Marcia so much and I'm very grateful to Neve as well – I just hope both ladies are happy with the final result!

My next big thank you is to my commissioning editor at The History Press, Mark Beynon. This has been a book seven years in the making and was due in 2013! For all that time, Mark gave me gentle nudges as to my progress. Towards the end, it was more a case of, 'Oh well, I live in hope' – just before the first chapters were sent in. Thanks, Mark – it would have been easy for you to wash your hands of this project, but your belief and persistence made me eventually fulfil my promise and also realise an ambition to write about Basil Rathbone.

Other people played a part in my research and I would like to express my gratitude to them: they include Kimi Ishikawa, whose father briefly worked for Basil; Alan Bennett for his help tracing ancestry of the Rathbone family; Major Ian Riley (retired) of the Liverpool Scottish Regiment; and Paul Stevens, librarian and archivist of Repton School. I'd also like to point out that the Repton School of Basil's time bears no relation to the highly regarded and respected school of the present day in any way, shape or form.

There have been others who have helped me enormously, and that's where Grace Clearsen comes in. Grace is the granddaughter of Basil Rathbone and she has provided a series of fascinating insights into Basil's life and relationship with her late father, Rodion. While Marcia and Neve laid the foundations for my investigations, Grace confirmed that the life Basil Rathbone projected publicly was different from the one he actually lived. Dounia Rathbone, great-granddaughter of Basil, also helped me along the way and for that I am very grateful.

As ever, I'd also like to thank my wife Sarah, and my three incredible kids Harry, Jaime and Chrissie. As Stephen King once said in a dedication, 'Promises to keep.'

Sadly, many of the actors that appeared with Basil in his many pictures and plays have passed away, but there was a treasure trove of memories in existence that I've knitted together, plus plenty of new revelations that I hope make this as fascinating to read as it was to write.

Make no mistake, Basil Rathbone is one of my favourite actors. For me, and millions of others around the world, it was his appearances as Sherlock Holmes that made me aware of his work. As a kid (and I know I'm not alone), I believed him to be a real person and was desperate to visit 221B Baker Street and see for myself the place the Great Detective had once called home.

When I began this biography, I had no idea just how many fantastic movies he had made or anything about his private life. He was a wonderful actor and the consummate professional with perhaps one of the greatest voices ever to grace showbusiness. But there will be times when you wonder how he did some of the things he did. Those moments are at odds with the warm and generous man whom so many people loved, and might have had a lot to do with the experiences and horrors he suffered during the war and his complicated and long marriage to Ouida Bergere. Those are judgements left to the reader to absorb and I doubt any two opinions will be the same. But I would add that there are so many instances and recollections of a warm and generous man in the pages that follow, which duel with some of the things Basil did in his life, that lead me to believe he must have deeply regretted certain moments in his life.

His portrayal of Sherlock Holmes will, in my view, never be bettered. He was the living embodiment of Sir Arthur Conan Doyle's masterful creation and Basil's Holmes movies have entertained millions for more than eighty years. Yet despite the exposure and wealth the role brought him, the relationship between actor and character would become torturous and the title of this book bears testament to that.

As Holmes himself once said, 'How often have I said that when you have excluded the impossible, whatever remains, however improbable, must be the truth?'

Prepare to exclude the impossible. The game is, indeed, afoot.

David Clayton
Cheshire, England
September 2019

Prologue

Who should play Holmes?! Basil Rathbone, of course!
Twentieth Century Fox producer/director
Gene Markey's response to who should play
the lead in *The Hound of the Baskervilles*

The life and times of Basil Rathbone could have comfortably filled the pages of any Sir Arthur Conan Doyle classic work of fiction. Intrigue, drama, tragedy, mystery, romance and a sprinkling of the macabre: Rathbone was many things to many people, but unravelling the enigma of one of the greatest British actors of his generation – perhaps of all time – would take the great detective Sherlock Holmes himself to solve.

War hero, son, brother, actor, husband, father, lover ... Basil Rathbone was all of these and more, yet the role he would eventually become synonymous with would also become his nemesis. Rathbone needed no Moriarty to continually torment him. In accepting the role of Sherlock Holmes, he had, in effect, cursed himself with a character he could never escape from professionally, and even when he attempted to effectively kill Holmes off, he suffered the same ignominy Conan Doyle had when he took the shock decision to finally see Holmes off once and for all in the infamous Reichenbach Falls incident. Millions of devoted fans of Holmes simply wouldn't accept his death and the writer was forced to backtrack, resurrect him and continue writing about his adventures with his faithful accomplice Dr Watson for thirty-four more years.

In time, Holmes would exact his own revenge on Rathbone who came to loathe a character he saw as one-dimensional, condescending, cold and mean spirited. Even worse, he despised the tacky, almost mocking recognition he received in everyday life that became almost unbearable for him. His efforts to extricate himself from the great detective were ultimately doomed to failure and there would only be one winner.

Rathbone the actor deserved better, and Rathbone the man deserved better. Many of his close friends believed the same – but there had been casualties along the way, and unlike the movies he starred in, not everything was black and white. In fact, so intertwined did character and actor become in public consciousness, that for many, Rathbone really was Sherlock Holmes, and few could tell where Holmes ended, and Rathbone began.

One thing is for certain. For Sherlock Holmes purists – and they are legion – there was only one actor who was the living, breathing embodiment of the character Sir Arthur Conan Doyle first unleashed on the world in the 1887 short story *A Study in Scarlet* – and that man was, indeed, Basil Rathbone.

1

1892–1906

The Talented Mr 'Ratters'

I am seeking, I am striving, I am in it with all my heart.

Vincent van Gogh

Philip St John Basil Rathbone was born on 13 June 1892, but the quintessential Englishman's birth was not in the green valleys of England, but Johannesburg where his mother and father had been working and living for several years.

His parents had married in 1891. Edgar Philip Rathbone hailed from the affluent Rathbone family of Liverpool who were non-conformist merchants, shipowners and also the owners of the Liverpool, London and Globe Insurance Company. In fact, Basil – as baby Philip St John would be known – was the great-grandson of the noted Victorian philanthropist, William Rathbone V. It was a family tradition not to use the first name, so the Rathbones' youngest child quickly became known as Basil.

Edgar was 36 years old when Basil was born, and his mother Anna, a talented violinist of Irish descent, was 25 when she gave birth to what was her first child. Edgar was a mine inspector and moved to Johannesburg along with many other professionals following the discovery of the Main Reef gold outcrop, which would see a sparsely populated area of South Africa become a vibrant hub, many attracted by the dreams of untold riches.

In all-too-familiar fashion, the news of a possible gold rush saw Johannesburg's population quickly swell to more than 100,000 people, and as with any imagined get-rich-quick opportunities, so too came a raft of philanderers, criminals, pimps, adventurers and crooks. The Rathbones were settled on the Trene Estate in Pretoria and Basil was baptised on 26 March 1894 at St Mary the Virgin Church in the Parish of Johannesburg, Diocese of Pretoria, with his sponsors listed as Thomas F. Carden, Frederick H. George and Helen Beatrice George – the latter related to his mother Anna, whose maiden name was also George.

In 1895, everything changed for the Rathbone family. After the Boers accused Edgar of being a British spy, the Rathbones were forced into a daring escape that would have read well in any spy novel. Years later, Basil would recount their dramatic escape as he wrote:

> Once again, under cover of darkness, we left our sanctuary. Upon arrival at the railroad station we found that train service had been considerably disrupted. There was however a freight train leaving in a couple of hours.
>
> The situation was too urgent to wait for a passenger train in the morning. So, we boarded a freight car and prepared for the long haul to Durban. It is some three hundred odd miles from Johannesburg to Durban, one hundred and twenty miles of which would be consumed in reaching the Natal Border – one hundred and twenty miles – and every mile fraught with danger to us all. We were fortunate in finding a car not too heavily loaded, in which there appeared to be adequate room for brief exercising should circumstances allow such a luxury. At one end of the car there was a small wooden seat. There my mother sat with her two children in her arms, while underneath it crouched my father, well hidden by the voluminous folds of my mother's skirt. Intermittently could be heard the sounds of voices and the coupling and uncoupling of cars

as the freight train was made up. Every start held the promise that we were on our way, and the hope that my father could take a brief respite from his cramped hiding place.

The drama was far from over for the Rathbone family, who may have arrived safely in Durban, but were in no fit state to travel further as Anna was sick and soon diagnosed as having typhoid fever. She was admitted to hospital, and a day later Basil and his sister fell foul of the same illness and all three were seriously ill for several weeks and under intensive medical care. It could have been the end of young Basil's adventure before it had really begun, but thankfully mother and children recovered fully and were finally ready to return to England.

They had wisely fled Johannesburg in a hurry and finally managed to make good their escape from South Africa, though there was one final twist. They had been booked to sail back to England on the Union Castle, but during Anna's delirious state in hospital she had suffered a nightmare so terrifyingly real that when she had recovered, she had begged Edgar not to sail on the ship in question. She had, in her mind, seen a portent of disaster so vivid, she was convinced it was a premonition of her family's death.

The dream saw a normal passage for the Union Star until it reached the Bay of Biscay, where it encountered a terrific storm. Not only did she see her family stranded as the ship began to list, but she heard the Seaforth Highlanders band playing 'Flowers of the Forest' as the ship started sinking – that's when she awoke, certain that her family were in mortal danger.

Sceptical, but understanding, Edgard switched the sailing to the Walmer Castle liner a week later. In Basil's autobiography, published in 1962, he writes that the Union Castle did indeed sink during a terrible storm in the Bay of Biscay, with all souls drowned as the Seaforth Highlanders band played 'Flowers in the Forest'. He said his mother could never have lied and his father backed up the story, but there is no obvious record of the Union Castle ship existing or a liner being lost at that time. Though Basil writes that the Union Castle Line shipping company could confirm these facts, they didn't come into existence until 1900, a few years after their voyage home. Perhaps the legend of the nightmare had grown and been embellished over the years in the family, to a point where it could no longer be undone. Or perhaps it was a different shipping company? Basil was only 4 at the time and when he wrote his memoirs, his parents had long since passed away. It's likely we'll never fully know the truth.

Regardless of the journey, the Rathbones were finally home and ready to settle into a new life in London. In later years, Basil recalled vague memories of the period and admitted he didn't know (or care) if his father really had been a spy or not because he had never asked him, though it is fair to say there was a mistrust and a certain amount of resentment from the Boers during the period the Rathbones and any other British citizens were in the country, mostly due to the First Boer War. Perhaps, in their eyes, all were the enemy, and all were spies. Whatever Edgar's real mission had been, it was all in the past now and it was time to move on.

Initially, the family lived at 145 Goldhurst Terrace in Hampstead, London. The residence was owned by a woman named Susannah Kinchingman, who was approximately 47 years old when the Rathbones took residence there, and for the 1901 Census Basil was listed as her son, though it is unclear why. Susannah was recorded as the 'Head of the house'. Today, the house, which still stands, is worth more than £1 million. It is most likely that, back then, it was a boarding house of some sort.

By 1901, Edgar was listed as a mining engineer and Basil spent his early years as a Londoner, taking great inspiration from his older cousin Frank Benson, a highly respected actor who had founded his own company and specialised in Shakespearian productions, many of which were based on long-forgotten or largely ignored tales from the great Bard. Benson was something of a hero to the juvenile Basil, who was fascinated by the theatre. It is fair to say that Benson was one of England's greatest classical actors of the time, and for thirty years he managed the Shakespearian Festival in Stratford-on-Avon, and though there is no proof as such, it is hard to think that an awestruck Basil didn't see some of his cousin's productions in London at some stage. Basil bore an uncanny resemblance to Frank Benson, too. Acting, it seemed, was very much in his DNA.

He enjoyed what he described as a 'very sweet' childhood. Younger brother John had been born and the family was complete, and they soon moved to their own property as Edgar found his feet again in London society. Basil's romantic leanings were evident even at a young age, when he began dating a girl called Esther who lived close by, and with her he shared his first kiss in the hayloft at the farm near to his home.

He spent idyllic Christmas holidays with his grandparents, and occasionally the family would visit their wealthy relatives at Greenbank Cottage in Wavertree, Liverpool, where he would again fall head over heels in love with their neighbour's daughter, Cynthia. Basil was a hopeless romantic, but he saw Cynthia dressed as a Fairy Queen and was completely smitten.

He knew her for just one day, dreaming of when he would see her again – but the next morning she had gone on holiday to Europe, and with his grandmother's passing not long after, he would never return to Greenbank Cottage again. But he never forgot Cynthia.

He wrote and directed a family production while at his grand-mother's residence – a pantomime – but as he'd written the best part and dialogue for himself, his siblings didn't put their heart and soul into the production! Still, it was his first attempt at what would eventually become his passion.

But a career in acting would have to wait and, aged 13, Basil had set his heart on public school, and one in particular: Repton, a long-established school some 140 miles north in Derbyshire. Basil knew of Repton's reputation as perhaps the foremost sporting school in the country at that time, and this was the driving force behind his determination to get there. He was a natural sportsman and a fierce competitor, so he was somewhat economical with the truth when insisting to his parents that Repton was the school where he would excel academically. Repton came at a price and it would be a sizeable financial commitment for his parents, but their support was never in question. Basil won a place at Repton, where he would board and stay during school term; however, he would keep the real reasons he was going there to himself. From September 1906 to April 1910, Basil was in a boarding house called Cattley's.

Already standing 6ft tall, Basil was a natural leader, and though he would struggle academically, Repton would allow him to thrive on the sports field. His sporting prowess quickly made him a popular figure amongst his peers, and this undoubtedly made his time at the school far more palatable than the fate of some of its less confident pupils.

Despite its reputation for education, sport and discipline, at the time it was a case of survival of the fittest at Repton, where bullying and 'fagging' – younger boys acting as servants to older boys – was a rife and even accepted tradition, with many of the masters turning a blind eye. Beatings, antisemitism and homosexual relationships were recorded in Repton's discipline log – also known as the 'Black Book' – and those who did suffer at the hands of others often underwent anguish and mental torment. Some years later, bestselling author Roald Dahl wrote of his experiences at Repton in his autobiographical tale *Boy*, claiming: 'All through my school life I was appalled by the fact that masters and senior boys were allowed literally to wound other boys, and sometimes quite severely... I couldn't get over it. I never have got over it.'

For Basil, however, life at Repton would be different. His four years there were afforded a chapter in his autobiography, *In and Out of Character*. Nicknamed 'Ratters', he seemed to relish his time as a Reptonian, and though he was devastated not to be selected to represent the school at cricket, his ability at football would elevate his status yet further. He recalled:

Football boots, well soaked in 'dubbin' against the invariably inclement weather – football boots with their masculine leather thongs... upon the notice board outside Pears' Hall – that magic word – 'Hopefuls'... one day my name was on that board... the first step towards one's colours.

Days when one had played badly – inspired days when one played with the thought of someday playing for England! Then, at last, that cold, wet afternoon when I.P.F Campbell, our captain, walked slowly towards me and took my hand on the football field. I had won my colours! A roar of young voices approving his choice, and a moment later, one was lifted on to the shoulders of one's friends and carted in triumph from the field of play. Later, one was to hear such applause again – many times – but no first night in any theatre anywhere held such ecstasy of accomplishment as that moment when one received one's colours at Repton School.

Naturally athletic, Basil's height, physique and speed ensured he would become a major asset for Repton's sporting reputation, though it was to the detriment of his education, where Basil admitted to putting his learning a firm second to the football field and athletic track. He wrote: 'I scraped through my exams, remaining pretty much at the bottom of my classes except for Carr and Vatchell, my bosom friends who I could rely upon to keep me out of bottom place.'

One sports day recorded in the school magazine has Basil finishing fourth in the steeplechase, while winning the 600m sprint and the Under-17s hurdles race. He also made it into the dreaded Black Book with the following entry: 'July 5th, 1909: Rathbone, Basil: Rowdy behaviour on Cricket Field on Sunday. Also disparaging Head Boy's warning and then lying about it. Flogged.'

Yet, when he did put his mind to it, Rathbone clearly had at least some academic ability, surprising both his teachers and friends by winning an essay competition – so much so, that his friends thought it must be a fluke! It also backfired somewhat in that it also convinced some of his masters that he was a 'slacker' who simply couldn't be bothered putting his heart and soul into education. The truth probably lay somewhere in between. He had already shown where his true passions lay and though he had the tools and imagination to succeed, he was all too aware that his other secret love – that of the theatre – would have changed his standing at the school entirely. As a sportsman, he was safe from the bullying and ridicule gentler, more artistic souls had been subjected to at Repton, and Basil had enough nous to keep his own thespian interests firmly to himself. He said:

Little did my friends realise that, during homework in the dining room, I was working on my first play, 'King Arthur'. Had my friends known, this would have indicated to them that I was not quite the 'he-man' they thought me to be. Repton was not a school that prided itself on the arts and any boy so interested would definitely be suspect of being a 'queer one'. And so, I kept my love of the theatre to myself.

It was a wise decision. Basil felt incredibly guilty about the financial hardship his parents suffered as a result of his schooling, hardships also felt by his younger siblings, sister Beatrice and brother John, though he said nobody in his family had held it against him and gave what they had 'affectionately and willingly'. The guilt stemmed from his academic results – or lack of – and the real reasons he'd wanted to attend Repton in the first place. Yet in many ways the decision was correct, as he was able to gain confidence, social standing, fulfil his competitive needs and achieve sporting prowess: assets that he would take and utilise into his future career – though, after leaving Repton behind, he would first have to negate his father's slightly more grounded vision of where his future employment lay…

2

1909–1916

Theatrical Release

Destiny is no matter of chance. It is a matter of choice. It is not a
thing to be waited for, it is a thing to be achieved.

William Jennings Bryan

Aged 17, and with his whole life in front of him, Philip St John Basil
Rathbone was ready to take on the world. His triumphant stay at
Repton had seen him carried through school largely on his athletic
prowess, with his academic achievements a very poor second.

Having successfully kept his love of acting and playwriting a secret,
he was now free of the masculine shackles he felt school had kept
him in during his time there, and was ready to follow his true calling.
His dream of becoming an actor was not dismissed by his parents, but
the sacrifices they'd made for their son to attend such a prestigious
place of learning needed some form of recompense and their teenage
son duly accepted as much. For now.

Frank Benson was the son of Basil's mother Anna's sister, and the
likeness to Basil was incredible. Edgar must have been aware of how
much Basil looked up to his older cousin – he was thirty-four years
his senior – and Benson's passion for Shakespeare. It was as though

Basil was Frank Benson junior, and Edgar and Anna probably realised their son would eventually follow his true calling to the stage, sooner rather than later.

Edgar had organised a position for Basil as a junior clerk at the Globe Insurance Company in London, where he was expected to learn the business and perhaps forge a steady career for himself. Dutifully, he accepted the role, no doubt feeling indebted to his parents and particularly his father, who had no doubt hoped his son's acting aspirations would eventually fade.

But there was little chance they would, and it was to be a fairly brief brush with the insurance world, with the budding actor desperate to forge a career of his own volition. Recalled Basil:

My father asked me to compromise by going into business for one year, at the end of which time I might do as I pleased. It was a generous compromise. And so, I became a junior clerk in the main office in London branch of the Globe Insurance Company and with him it was made clear that I was due for early promotion, provided I worked hard. I was given special instruction and attended lectures after hours, and within a few months I was moved to the accounting department of the West End Branch at Charing Cross, under the local management of E. Preston Hytch – a bald-headed, hard-working Dickensian, with very little discipline over his staff. During this period, I was elected to play cricket and football, every Saturday afternoon for the L, L & G's first team. I was also invited to spend a weekend with Mr and Mrs Lewis and their eligible daughter. It was all so obvious and made no impression on me, except to increase my determination to be rid of them all at the end of the one year.

On 22 April 1911, he finally got the opportunity he'd been waiting for. Using his family connections, he won the part of Hortensio in Sir Frank Benson's No. 2 Company production of *The Taming of the Shrew* at the Theatre Royal in Ipswich. The No. 2 company was made up of promising young talent, still finding their feet, but it was a highly respected branch of the Benson empire – a sort of academy of aspiring actors.

Directed by Henry Hubert, the teenage Rathbone impressed sufficiently to be invited on a tour of the United States with Benson's troop in October 1912. The chance to take Shakespeare to the States, and playing roles such as Paris in *Romeo and Juliet*, Fenton in *The Merry Wives of Windsor* and Silvius in *As You Like It*, was impossible to turn down. He was doing what he loved, earning a living and travelling the world as he honed his craft. The trip to the United States would also be the beginning of a lifelong love with a country he would eventually call home in years to come. Basil was in his element and thrived on tour, winning wide acclaim for a striking performance in *A Midsummer Night's Dream*. Like cousin Frank, he was a devoted student of Shakespeare and this was his destiny. Everything, it seemed, was going to plan.

With Benson's Shakespeare Festival in Stratford-upon-Avon still going strong, Basil would appear in many varied productions as he shaped into the classical actor that would bring wealth and fame in later life. It was also there that he would meet actress Marion Foreman, with whom he would fall hopelessly in love. In his autobiography, Rathbone wrote:

Marion had been on stage for some time before I met her in Stratford in August 1913. She was an excellent actress with a beautiful speaking and singing voice. We were cast opposite one another in 'second leads' such as Lorenzo and Jessica in *The Merchant of Venice* and Silvius and Phoebe in *As You Like It*. Both on and off the stage we saw much of each other for many months.

Marion was five years Basil's senior, and as the romance blossomed so did his acting career. On 9 July 1914, the 22-year-old actor finally played in his home city for the first time, portraying the part of Finch in *The Sin of David* at the Savoy Theatre in the West End. The sky, it seemed, was the limit for the gifted young actor, as he effortlessly recited Shakespearian classics in front of packed theatres around the country. Indeed, 'Ratters' would have been unrecognisable to his former classmates at Repton, who might have imagined he would go on to play football, cricket or compete as an athlete at a much higher level once he left school. With that in mind, perhaps he had already tucked one of his finest acting roles under his belt?

However, the path to fame and fortune would need to be temporarily – perhaps permanently – put to one side. In Europe, major storm clouds were gathering on the horizon, and towards the end of July Britain joined France and Russia in the Triple Entente Coalition, while Germany, Austria and Italy formed the opposing Triple Alliance as the July Crisis saw escalating and diplomatic arguments rage between some of Europe's most powerful nations. What had seemed inevitable soon became reality, with the disputes eventually leading to the start of what would eventually become the First World War and the most devastating human conflict the planet had ever witnessed.

Time and tide wait for no man, and perhaps sensing the enormity of the conflict in Europe, by the autumn Basil and Marion were married. The wedding announcement read:

October 3rd, 1914: Church of St Luke Parish of Battersea London, Philip St. John Basil Rathbone age 22 bachelor, professional actor, of 24 Hendrick Avenue. Father: Edgar Philip Rathbone occupation mining engineer wed Ethel Marion Forman, age 27 spinster on profession, of 29 Bassaley Road, Newport, Wales, daughter of Edward Forman, occupation member of the British College of Physical Education. In the presence of Barbara Rathbone and Edward Forman.

Marion, it seems, was always inhabiting a role of some sort, and friend Babs Richards of her hometown of Newport recalled: 'I knew Marion very well. She always dressed in black and one felt she was always giving a performance, even when she [was] just speaking to you. She directed many plays, mainly outdoor productions of Shakespeare.'

Basil and Marion seemed a perfect match, and soon the arts-loving newlywed couple were expecting their first child. Or had they discovered the pregnancy first and then decided to get married? Only they knew the truth. Marion would give birth nine months later, so conception had either happened immediately, or they had indeed known beforehand and hastily wed.

A few months later, Basil appeared as The Dauphin in *Henry V* at the Shaftesbury Theatre, and he continued to tour throughout 1915 with Benson's No. 2 Company, with whom he was now considered one of the troop's lead players, but he was also at war with his own inner turmoil. He had become a father for the first time in July 1915, Marion giving birth to a healthy boy they named Rodion, and things were going well for the Rathbones, but Basil's beloved younger brother John had wasted no time and joined the army straight from school a few months before Rodion's birth. By June 1915, John was appointed captain in the Dorset Regiment, 3rd Battalion, and if anything tipped the balance for Basil it was perhaps the thought that his kid brother was fighting for his country and risking his life every day while he continued to entertain in theatres around the country.

As the war cast an ever-greater shadow over the daily lives of the British, so Basil wrestled with his own conscience – to enlist, or stay out of it for as long as possible and hope for the best? He may have been born in South Africa, but his heart and soul belonged to England, and with that came an all-too-British stiff upper lip that was driving him towards an inevitable conclusion. His torment was evident when he wrote: 'I felt physically sick to my stomach, as I saw or heard or read of the avalanche of brave young men rushing to join… while I was pondering how long I could delay joining up.'

Captain John Rathbone was hugely popular among his men, and like his older brother was clearly a natural leader of men. Charismatic and affable, he was proud to serve his country, though would never have questioned his Basil's reticence, particularly as he now had a wife and baby son to care for – but Basil finally made his decision and on 30 March 1916, with his son not yet 10 months old, he decided he could stand by and watch no longer as thousands of men gave their lives for king and country. His acting career was officially put on hold – maybe permanently – and his role as husband and father indefinitely paused.

Before his life in the military began in earnest, Basil recalled a proud moment for his beloved cousin and the unusual manner in which he became a Knight of the Realm. He wrote:

Sir Frank Benson was knighted at Drury Lane Theatre on Tuesday, May 2, 1916, at a special Royal Command performance of *Julius Caesar* in which every part, even 'walk-ons,' were played by stars or well-known actors. After his death as *Julius Caesar*, Mr Benson was commanded to the royal box. There, with all eyes on him, in his toga, dripping with blood, he knelt before King George V and received the accolade. There was an amusing moment when King George asked for a sword. There was a considerable pause – no word was spoken between the King and Mr Benson, who remained kneeling. Then at last a jewelled-handled sword was produced from somewhere and the naked blade rested first on Mr Benson's left shoulder then on his right, as King George spoke the magic words, 'Rise, Sir Frank Benson.' There was a roar of applause.

Less than four months after that proud moment, Sir Frank's son Eric William Benson was killed in the Battle of the Somme, aged 29.

Basil was not yet 24, but the time was right. If not literally fighting alongside his brother, he would fight the same battle, and together they could try and outwit the same enemy and hope they would both return home triumphant into the arms of those who loved them. What Marion thought of the whole situation, one can only guess, but it was a time when the women of Britain staunchly stood by their men – and what more noble a cause could there be than fighting for the liberty of others and to bring an end to what was a horrific conflict? Rathbone makes no reference to what must have been an incredibly difficult period in his life in his autobiography, only that he would look back on that particular period with great regret. In some ways, though neither he nor Marion knew it at that time, their marriage was ending before it had really begun, with Basil, who had openly admitted he was 'appalled' by the thought of soldiering and could not understand why so many would join up by their own free will, now part of the same war machine he so despised. Like everything else in his life up to that point, if he was in, he was in, and he would be totally committed to the cause. There were no half-measures for Basil Rathbone – it was all or nothing.

He attended basic training in Richmond Park, just outside London, and it was here that Private Rathbone learned how to hate and, if he had to, kill the enemy. Spared an almost immediate call-up to the northern battlefields of France (which was not uncommon for newly trained recruits), Basil decided to apply to become a commissioning officer, and to his surprise was accepted and sent to an officers' training camp in Gailes, Scotland. Certain aspects of life at Gailes reminded Rathbone of Repton and he was once again allowed to indulge his love of sport. After meeting a kindred spirit in a Scottish rugby international he refers to only as 'MacDonald', both men were soon rallying the cadets into 'Blues' and 'Reds', one side led by MacDonald, the other by Rathbone. They competed fiercely in football, rugby and athletics, raising morale and both almost unknowingly displaying their considerable leadership skills in the process. The camp was alive, the competitiveness and camaraderie at an all-time high, but the ghosts of Repton were still evident for Private Rathbone – academically, both MacDonald and Basil were heading for failure in the impending officer exams.

However, their efforts outside the classroom had not gone unnoticed, and when Gailes's chief, Captain Smith, hauled them both into his office to warn them of their impending fate, he did so in an advisory capacity and not a chiding way – make no mistake, he knew both men were perfect and inspirational leaders of men, but rules were rules and they had to meet at least the most basic academic standards. He sat them down in his office and told them exactly what they needed to do:

Look ... I've been watching you very closely since you arrived, and it didn't take me long to realise you both have unusual qualities of leadership. The army in France needs men like you and I am going to see to it you get your commissions – but on one condition. You fellows are going to swat like dogs these next three weeks to come up with creditable exam papers. It's up to you, so get going and don't let me down. And I don't give a damn who wins the damned football final. Dismissed!

For the record, Rathbone's team – the Blues – won, both men studied hard to bring their grades to a just about acceptable level, and both were passed as commissioned officers. Basil, as requested, was sent to the Liverpool Scottish Battalion and he and MacDonald went their separate ways. The games were well and truly over and there was no turning back from here on in ...

3

1917–1918

An Officer and a Gentleman

Courage is the commitment to begin without any guarantee of success.

Johann Wolfgang Von Goethe

The area in between the German trenches and the British trenches was, of course, known as No Man's Land. Completely exposed, soldiers were forced to cross No Man's Land in order to advance. It was extremely dangerous and slow going due to barbed wire, land mines and machine-gun fire from the enemy trenches. In addition, the muddy, sodden ground was often littered with the decaying bodies of soldiers who had unsuccessfully attempted to cross it.

The British soldiers typically spent about a week or two living in the trenches and fighting on the front line. Then another unit would replace them on the front line, and the first unit would go 'out of the line' to spend a week or so resting in a nearby village. This brief rest period gave the soldiers an opportunity to eat regular meals and get regular sleep, so they'd be ready for another round of fighting

Basil Rathbone never wanted to be part of the conflict, but he had a sense of duty and was undoubtedly as committed as the next man.

Contrary to his fears of enlisting, Basil had decided that if push came to shove, he would give his life serving his country and was prepared to fall on his sword if it was for the benefit of his men.

There was reticence and fear, as there were for millions of youngsters entering a battle they knew they might never return from, but there was also courage and determination by the bucketload. His academic limitations at school and during officer training were due to nothing more than a lack of interest and application. His skills lay in leadership and the ability to rally those around him into an enthusiastic, collective unit who shared the same goal. In short, he was perfect officer material and exactly what the army were looking for.

Having been assigned to The Liverpool Scottish, 2nd Battalion, Rathbone was prepared for war and all that came with it. The unit had been attached to the 57th Division, but for reasons that are unclear, they would be held back in England for several months as they awaited their instructions. Perhaps the War Office believed a German invasion was possible and wanted soldiers capable of defending the land if caught by surprise, or at least holding back the enemy until reinforcements arrived – whatever the reason, it meant, for the time being, that they were staying put. This allowed the men to fully bond and Second Lieutenant Rathbone to grow into the role he had been given.

He wrote:

I was no longer in a position to consider myself. I was in command of a platoon of men who were almost completely dependent on me in every possible way and who looked on me for example and leadership, whatever the circumstances. I became very fond of my men and I like to think they were very fond of me.

It would be several months before the order came through, and during that time Basil's younger brother John was wounded at the Somme, though his injuries were thankfully not life-threatening and once recovered, he would return to battle. Basil was further delayed from the conflict when he contracted measles in February 1917 and stayed at 24 Hendrick Avenue close to Wandsworth Common in London while he recovered. Here he shared the house with his brother John.

John was still recovering from the wounds he had received the previous July. He had been shot through the chest and right lung, and it must have given the brothers great comfort to be together again, even if only for a month or so. As soon as Basil was better, he returned to the depot and trained again with the men under his command. He soon felt thoroughly adjusted to army life and, two months later, was finally sent abroad to join his battalion, the 2/10 Battalion King's Liverpool Regiment, in the trenches near Bois-Grenier. On 23 May 1917, the unit's war diary refers to the battalion being in billets. It also notes that a '2nd Lt P St J Rathbone' had reported for duty and duly posted to B Company.

Rathbone had had a somewhat unemotional departure from the train station, with his parents, he surmised, perhaps putting on a brave face. They had already seen one son injured and they were all-too-aware they could lose both John and Basil in the months ahead. Parents and son, it seems, had conditioned themselves for that particular moment, and though Basil felt his father's true feelings were closer to the surface than his mother's, the goodbyes were as they would have been for any other journey.

'It's just like seeing Basil off to Repton in the old days, isn't it, Edgar?' remarked his mother.

His father forced a smile. 'Write as soon and as often as you can son, won't you?'

The troop train left Victoria Station for Folkestone and things would never be the same for the Rathbone family. Basil would never see his mother again as she died not long after seeing her son off to war. The strain it undoubtedly caused her contributed to her untimely passing, aged only 51.

Basil settled to life in the army well, and by June 1918 was the patrols officer for his battalion. There were rumours, disinformation and suspicion regarding the enemy and an urgency to obtain covert information on the Germans. Word had spread that they were pulling out of their positions, with transport movements in the dead of night appearing to confirm as much. If they were, why? What were their plans? Was an attack imminent? High Command had only limited intelligence available. The events to that point had seen Lieutenant Rathbone take all in his stride, but suddenly everything was polarised, and he knew he had to do something: make things happen.

With the Germans dug in opposite, the best that could be done up to that point was brief forays by reconnaissance patrols into No Man's Land during darkness. These afforded little intelligence and the prize of capturing a German soldier was almost an impossibility, with both factions understandably reluctant to engage at close quarters. Rathbone's unit were seasoned soldiers who, he believed, knew how to manipulate certain situations in order to reduce the risk of confrontation. They weren't afraid or lazy – far from it – but they knew if they made reports of a potential enemy patrol anywhere nearby, the chain of action that followed invariably meant waiting for further instruction from the commanding officer, and so followed a delay while the processes kicked in. Every moment you didn't have shells exploding in close proximity or bullets flying at you was time well spent. It was a tried and tested protocol that had to be observed and considered, and reports written.

Basil wrote:

> Some of the reports I wrote were based on fact, but some were pure fiction! As I recall, many of them were masterpieces of invention; inconclusive, yet suggesting every effort had been made by our patrol to garner and/-or make contact with the enemy. Under such circumstances, one's imagination was often sorely tried in supplying acceptable 'news items' that could be examined at Battalion HQ and then confidently filed away under the heading 'Intelligence'.

He had tired of the predictability of their situation, the daily monotony and routine, and decided it was time to make things happen rather than sit and wait. The events that unfolded next would have served him well as a dramatic lead role in his future Hollywood career – one of those parts would invariably be remarked upon that things like that 'only happened in the movies'. It would also lead Basil to winning one of the highest honours the armed forces could bestow. His plan was to profit from what he called 'the Germans' lack of imagination'. Had this been a game of chess, it had reached an impasse with each side fairly certain of the other's next move – so much so that Rathbone concocted a plan entirely based on such familiarity, which would become the enemy's undoing. He was to take the Germans by surprise via a series of surreptitious advances. Neither side were going to send daylight patrols out due to the proximity of the other and so, considered Rathbone, if the Germans' guard was effectively relaxed during this time, was it then not the best time to take advantage? He informed his commanding officer, Colonel Monroe, that he planned to take a sniper into No Man's Land at the break of day, just as the dawn sentry was changing over. He figured that if ever there was a time of opportunity, it would be between the handover from the night watch to the daytime watch. Moreover, he felt the Germans' reputation for being sticklers for precision and daily routine would almost guarantee the chance to make ground towards their trenches virtually unnoticed. He would, in effect, be hiding in plain sight.

To achieve this, he returned to his theatrical experience and suggested both he and his sniper should be heavily camouflaged. He recalled:

The 'ham' in me suddenly became stronger than my sense of survival. Colonel Monroe seemed intrigued and gave his consent. The following morning, I was awoken by my batman at 3.30am. Camouflage suits had been made for us to resemble trees and on our heads, we wore wreaths of freshly picked foliage, our faces and hands were blackened with burnt cork. At about 5am we crawled through our wire and lay up in no-man's land. All sentries had been alerted to our movements. The German trenches were some 200 yards distant.

The risk was immense, bordering on a suicide mission, yet each day he went out at dawn with Corporal Tanner, edging a little further towards the German trenches undetected. During their reconnaissance, they identified the positions of the German machine guns and these were duly put out of action. Rathbone also noted their front-line positions were sparsely populated, giving credence to the High Command suspicion that something was indeed underway or about to happen. But more intelligence was needed. They needed solid, hard evidence, and Rathbone was prepared to risk his life to get it with a staggering act of bravery that must have felt like an almost impossible mission. After Colonel Monroe suggested that either a raid or the capturing of a prisoner were the only two options, Rathbone said he would breach the German defences alone with his trusted sniper.

He was banking on the shock of appearing in their trenches in broad daylight being sufficient for him to get in and out in time and take the information back with him. The following morning, he and Corporal Tanner again advanced into No Man's Land, heavily camouflaged. But this time things would be different, and as they slowly crawled across the muddy, pitted ground, a squadron of German airplanes dived over their heads.

For a moment, Rathbone was lost in awe at the sight that met his eyes:

> Each plane was a different colour. The leading plane was black, and its pilot was the famous Baron van Richtofen – the second was painted red and its pilot was Herman Goering. The other planes were painted blue, green, yellow and so on, but as far as I know, their pilots never became as famous as their leaders. The squadron passed over us not more than 100 feet up, strafing the British who returned their fire, while from the German lines, there were cheers upon cheers.

Rathbone detected an almost festive atmosphere from enemy lines and the planes were soon gone, leaving him to consider the whole unreal situation he found himself in, witnessing one of the era's great-est air displays while effectively disguised as parkland bush, exposed for all the world to see – except still nobody had seen them. If any-thing, the squadron's appearance worked perfectly in Rathbone's favour as he figured if ever the distracted Germans' guard would have been down, it would be now. 'Let's go,' he whispered to Tanner.

They crawled for another hour and headed between two machine-gun posts, and on reaching their goal Rathbone stood up to test the water. If he'd been spotted, he would be dead in seconds. Instead, there was nothing, and he and Tanner cut the wires and rolled into the German front line where they remained motionless for several minutes, assessing and absorbing every sight and sound. Gradually, they made their way along the trench, turning a corner which was also empty of men. Then, as they continued stealthily and turned the next corner, they heard footsteps approaching. Suddenly, a German soldier was now facing them, frozen in shock and surprise at what he probably believed to be an impossibility. Two British soldiers, decked out as shrubbery, stood facing him in his own trench. Rathbone took a millisecond to realise there was no way he could capture the soldier, and so he quickly drew his revolver and shot him twice. He fell, dead, and Tanner removed his identification tags while Rathbone rifled his pockets and found a folded piece of paper and a diary.

They could hear the approach of more soldiers, so they quickly left the trench and ran through the barbed wire, Rathbone badly gashing his leg as he did so, but they made it to the first shell hole intact just seconds before the machine guns opened fire. With still 100 yards to go to safety, Rathbone had to think on his feet as bullets peppered their makeshift shelter. It came to him quickly and he surmised a plan to get both him and his sniper back safely. The plan was simplicity itself. He would run to the next shell hole on his left, Tanner to the next one on his right. He banked that the Germans wouldn't know whom to target first – and, unbelievably, it worked. Though a mile apart by the time they returned to their own trenches, Rathbone and Tanner had made it back safely and the information they returned with confirmed the suspicions that the Germans were retreating. While his men congratulated him on his successful mission, one commented that he smelled rank. No wonder. During the run back to safety, Rathbone had stepped in the rotting carcass of a dead soldier. It was only now that the gravity of the situation, his daring raid and the fact he had shot and killed another man hit him hard. He had been running on pure adrenaline the entire time – probably for days – and he was mentally and physically exhausted. Father, husband, son, sportsman, actor, soldier, spy… Rathbone was all of these and more, and he was also now a war hero who would later be awarded the Military Cross for his incredible and selfless act of bravery.

But there was tragedy awaiting, just a few days away. And Basil was certain it was coming.

4

1918

Night Terrors

'A single death is a tragedy; a million deaths is a statistic.'

Joseph Stalin

Over the course of his life, Basil Rathbone demonstrated what could be described as a mixture of psychic and clairvoyant abilities. Almost always, his visions were tragic and foretold death, almost instantaneous as the deaths actually occurred. It troubled him greatly, and though they were thankfully rare, when the psychic episodes came, they were powerful, shocking and terrifyingly real.

Basil's reward for his successful mission into enemy lines was to be billeted at a peaceful countryside farmhouse in the small village of Festubert for some much-needed rest and recuperation, where his mood immediately lifted from the horror of the previous days of careful advancement, concentration and, ultimately, killing another man at close quarters. Under blissful blue skies, with birds singing in the warm summer sunshine, for the first time in many months he was able to completely relax and, in his own words, 'allow for some self-indulgencies'. Feeling a world away from the unrelenting horrors of the conflict, Rathbone enjoyed a dreamless, deep sleep and ate a hearty breakfast the following morning. His hosts, a pig farmer and his wife, spoke no English, but with his guard down, the English soldier fell almost immediately in love with their beautiful daughter, Marie.

He recalled:

> She was the first pretty girl I had seen for a long time – and the results were disastrous. I couldn't sleep and all the next day I waited for the moment I would see her again. Her mother never left us alone – her mother, who sat at the other end of the kitchen table – watching and listening and breathing heavy garlic fumes over us both. I shall never know what Marie thought and felt about me, as she could not understand English and I was afraid to talk to her in French in case her mother should understand my intentions.

The hot-blooded soldier and virtuous farm girl made for a charged atmosphere, and in the days that followed Rathbone attempted to climb a tree to her bedroom for perhaps just a few moments alone, where he could no doubt profess his undying love. But his efforts would fail comically. He clambered up to where he believed Marie's room to be, only to instead tap on the window that belonged to her mother, who opened it and asked who was out there, followed by her husband who asked the same! The branch he was resting on duly broke and he crashed to the ground, thankfully hurting only his pride in the fall. It was perhaps then that he accepted that whatever this was, it was simply not meant to be. Maybe forces were at work outside his control, and the events of the next few weeks and months would suggest that possibility might not have been as outlandish as it sounds.

The next day, he received a welcome telephone call from his younger brother John, by now recovered from his injuries and back on the front line. John's Dorset Regiment was stationed close by. He wanted to come and stay with Basil for the evening, so the pair could catch up on what seemed like an age of time that had passed by since their last meeting in London. After Colonel Monroe gave his consent, John travelled to see his brother back at the London Scottish Mess. John was a hugely likeable character and Basil noted that in just one night, he had made himself as popular and well-liked as he was within his own regiment. After drinking 'good whisky and eating fine food', Basil and John slept in the same single bed and were soon sound asleep. Then, Basil awoke with a start. The room was still pitch black and all was quiet, but Basil was in a state of mild panic. In the nightmare he had just endured, he had seen John killed, and he felt that what he had seen was a vision of what was to be, not a dream. He held a candle to light John's face and check he was still breathing, and was relieved to see he was soundly asleep. He gently kissed him on the head and went back to rest, still dreadfully troubled by the dream. It was a premonition so powerful that he was unable to entirely banish it from his thoughts. The next day, as John was about to leave, he embraced his brother tightly and the pair spoke of their plans to celebrate once the war had ended. It was a meeting that would never take place.

Rathbone wrote:

Some weeks later, at one o'clock on June 4, 1918, I was sitting in my dugout on the front line. Suddenly, I thought of John and for some inexplicable reason, I wanted to cry, and did. Immediately, I wrote him a letter to which he never replied, and in due course, I received news of his death in action at exactly one o'clock on June the fourth. We had always been very close to one another.

The horrific premonition had not only come true, but John's death had happened at the precise moment he had come into Basil's head, causing him to weep uncontrollably for no apparent reason. First his mother, now his beloved younger brother. The war was tearing the Rathbone family apart, both directly and indirectly. A letter Basil wrote to his grieving father and sister Beatrice reveals his anger at his brother's death:

July 26th
Wed morning

Dear father –

We came up from the reserves a while ago, and just before we left, I had your letter and also the parcel from uncle H. Please thank uncle and all the family especially the girls for their dear little poems. The whisky has already proved helpful. I shared the cake with my men, and it was consumed in three minutes and pronounced to be pretty fair, which is high praise.

I'm sorry for the awful handwriting but it's very cold and I'm shivering terribly and there's only an inch of candle left in the dugout to write by and it flickers. It's 3.50am, so bitterly cold I'm wearing my great coat though it's July, but it's been a quiet night, and when I was out, I caught a nice moon, very bright between little bits of cloud. I think it will be a very bright and sweet and warm day again like yesterday. Cloudless and a little breeze. Just the day for cricket.

Today will be quite a busy one and so I want to send this before it gets going.

I have all of Johnny's letters parcelled up together and I will either bring them home on my next leave or arrange for someone to deliver them in person. I would send them as you asked, but I would be afraid of them being lost. The communication trenches can take a beating, and nothing can be relied on. If I can't bring them myself for any reason there is a good sort here, another Lieutenant in our company who is under oath to deliver them, and who I have never known to shirk or break his word. So, you will get them, come what may.

I'm sorry not to have written much the past weeks. It was unfair and you are very kind not to be angry. You ask how I have been since we heard, well, if I am honest with you, and I may as well be, I have been seething. I was so certain it would be me first of either of us. I'm even sure it was supposed to be me, and he somehow contrived in his wretched Johnny-fashion to get in my way just as he always would when he was small. I want to tell him to mind his place. I think of his ridiculous belief that everything would always be well, his ever-hopeful smile, and I want to cuff him for a little fool. He had no business to let it happen and it maddens me that I shall never be able to tell him so or change it or bring him back. I can't think of him without being consumed with anger at him for being dead and beyond anything I can do to him.

I'm afraid it's not what you hoped for from me and perhaps that's why I haven't written. I suspect you want me to say some sweet things about him. I wish I could for your sake, but I don't have them to say. Out here we step over death every day. We stand next to it while we drink our tea. It's commonplace and ordinary. People who had lives and tried to hold on to them and didn't, and now slump and stare and melt slowly to nothing. You meet their eyes, or what used to be their eyes and you feel ashamed. And now Johnny is one of them. That's an end of it. Grieving is only ridiculous in this place. It could be me today or tomorrow and I shouldn't want anyone to bother grieving over that.

PSB (Philip St John Basil)

And there was to be more sadness. A few weeks later, Basil was informed that the area around Marie's farmhouse had been heavily shelled by the Germans and he made known his intention to make the journey there to see the devastation for himself, hoping that if her family had been affected, he could perhaps in some way help them. He was allowed to borrow the colonel's horse and made the short journey to Festubert in torrential rain to be met by a scene of utter devastation. The farmhouse had been reduced to nothing more than a pile of rubble and there was no sign of Marie or her parents. The only life he noted on this once thriving farm was a stray dog scavenging for food. He made enquiries nearby, but nobody knew what had become of the pig farmer's family. It was yet another blow to a man who had endured his share of tragedy in the past year or so. Crestfallen, he returned to base, apologised for the condition of the horse and asked the colonel to be excused from the Mess that evening.

His good will and positive outlook had been continually eroded and his only thoughts now were of home and an end to the war.

In later years, he would succinctly sum up his true feelings of war and there was nothing, in his eyes, that was either noble or brave about the years he spent fighting the Germans. He said:

> Going into an attack, paralyzed with fear, knowing that if we had our own free will, not a living man of us would go! Every living man of us would funk it. We go because we cease to be individuals. We become a mass machine. We are dominated by mass psychology. We become a composite thing of arms, legs, heads and wills. We move into the attack only because it is the only way out. If we do not go into the attack, if we turn back one quivering inch, we are shot down like dogs – deserters. So, we are forced to go forward, not because we are brave and gallant gentlemen, but because we are in a trap. War is a trap, a monstrous, gigantic, inconceivably barbarous trap. And there you have it. A trap is the most horrible thing in the world. Any kind of a trap. Because in a trap you are alone, crouched there with fear. There is Death screaming at you in front. There is Death sticking his tongue out at you from behind. In the trap a man, no longer a man, lives with Death. There is no horror like it!

Before he could return home, Basil was deservedly rewarded for his bravery, leadership and ingenuity when on 9 September 1918, he was awarded the Military Cross – an honour 'bestowed upon commissioned and warrant officers for distinguished and meritorious service in battle'. For additional acts of bravery, a straight silver bar was awarded, and during the First World War only 2,885 of these medals were awarded to British officers. The citation for Rathbone included the following:

> Lieutenant Rathbone volunteered to go out on daylight patrol, and on each occasion brought back invaluable information regarding enemy's posts, and the exact position and condition of

the wire. When on the enemy's side of the wire, he came face to face with a German. He shot the German, but this alarmed two neighbouring posts, and they at once opened a heavy fire with two machine guns. Despite the enemy fire, Lieutenant Rathbone got his man and himself through the enemy wire and back to our lines. The result of his patrolling was to pin down exactly where the enemy posts were, and how they were held, while inflicting casualties on the enemy at no loss to his own men. Lieutenant Rathbone has always shown a great keenness in patrol work both by day and by night.

Within a few weeks of receiving his medal, his wish had finally come true. The 'war to end all wars', with a global estimate of 16 million people killed during the brutal conflict, was finally over. He was going home, but would be doing so with a heavy heart. He had lost John, seen any potential future with Marie destroyed, and his father was now a widower – and, by all accounts, something of a lost soul without Basil's mother by his side. His sister Beatrice, in many ways, was also lost to the war, having lost her mother and younger brother during the conflict. She was a different woman and would never be the same again. In effect, the war had torn their close, loving family into shreds.

Still a married man with a 3-year-old son he had barely seen since birth to consider, Basil was full of inner turmoil as he made the short sailing back to England. He was uncertain he would ever resurrect his acting career and was almost certainly suffering from post-traumatic stress disorder, but this was not a known or recognised condition at that time. Soldiers in a haze or psychologically damaged were deemed to have 'shell shock' and expected to snap out of it at some stage. Though there were brief celebrations that the war had ended among his men, the journey home was to be a pensive, sombre passage with many soldiers deep in thought at all they had witnessed and the many friends, family and colleagues they had lost over the past four years. Many wept as the white cliffs of Dover came into view as the enormity of the past few years struck them.

But Basil had changed. The carefree, focused man he had been before war had gone, and like many other returning from the conflict, the terrors he had experienced meant it would take time to readjust to normal life. Sadly that meant he was in no fit state to be a husband and father to Marion and son Rodion.

He would later recall:

> I had come back from the war, where life had been like a long, terrible dream. At the front I had never thought about what would happen or why. There was no past and no future. Nights were either wet nights or dry nights. The important things to me were whether my billet was warm or cold, the food good or rotten. I suppose when you meet death daily for a long time you give up trying to order things. I came out of the war comparatively untouched. That is, I wasn't shell-shocked or scarred up. But I had lost all sense of life's realities. I found I was still a good enough actor. I got some good parts in London. Whatever they offered me, I took. Money meant nothing to me. I never thought of getting ahead. I never cared about it. Somehow, I expected to be taken care of – as I had been in the army. I shrank from decisions. I never went after things I wanted. I hated any sort of battle or argument. I just wanted to be let alone – to vegetate. I was completely negative.

Inevitably, after less than a year of life back in London, Basil and Marion separated. He had little or no motivation for anything and the future looked decidedly bleak if he couldn't rediscover his love of acting. He needed to rediscover himself, and perhaps distance himself from the life he had once had and start afresh. Marion and Rodion became the latest casualties of the war which continued ruining lives and families long after it had finished.

5

1920–1922

Onwards and Forwards

If I must start somewhere, right here and now is the best place imaginable.

Richelle E. Goodrich

Marion Rathbone refused to believe her separation from Basil was permanent rather than temporary, believing her husband needed time to readjust to normal life again after the horrors of war. He had left the family home and was living in a small flat in London, though he made sure he provided financial support to his wife and son as the parting had been his decision and he didn't see why they should suffer because of it.

The problem was he was not earning the sort of money that could keep two households going. He continued to accept roles that were, frankly, beneath him, but they helped keep his head above water and allowed him to ease back into acting.

Though he felt it had been right to leave Marion, he struggled with guilt, writing: 'Self-condemnation fought bitterly with self-justification, and there was no one to turn to and talk with about such intimate personal matters... my son was missing his father.'

The occasional work here and there turned into a steady stream of plays in London and Stratford-upon-Avon, where his reputation as one of England's most promising actors was gathering momentum. In 1919 he appeared at the Shakespeare Summer Festival at the Memorial Theatre in Stratford. He also appeared in *Julius Caesar*, *The Tempest*, *The Winter's Tale*, *Romeo and Juliet*, *The Merry Wives of Windsor* and *A Midsummer Night's Dream*. He returned to London to appear in *Napoleon*, *The Merchant of Venice*, *A Night on the Trojan Walls* and *Calliwachus*.

During his portrayal of Romeo in Stratford, perhaps inevitably given his habit of falling deeply in love very quickly, he began spending time with his co-star who played Juliet – a young actress called Joyce Carey. Perhaps the feeling of being back on the boards and doing what he loved, plus the dreamy Stratford surroundings and the balmy summer weather all played their part, too. Rathbone wrote:

> How could a still impressionable young man not fall in love with his Juliet? To me she was Juliet. And many who saw us perform maintain we more perfectly represented these star-crossed lovers than any other couple in living memory… After the play, Juliet and I would sail away up the Avon in a punt and partake of supper under the weeping willow trees – or walk through the fields and woods of Shakespeare's country until the early hours of the morning.
>
> Joyce was nineteen at the time, I think – a lovely child whose Juliet had a piquant expectancy about it that I had never met before. We saw a great deal of each other and lived in an atmosphere of the play, walking together on moonlight nights over to Shottery where Shakespeare had courted Ann Hathaway, or we would seek the seclusion of the willow-laden riverbanks or the silent inspiring little streets of Stratford herself.

Basil had immersed himself in the romance of one of Shakespeare's most celebrated plays and was effectively living the part of Romeo. Given the surrounds, it is hardly surprising that life was imitating art and he went along with it completely. Basil would continue to see and work with Joyce over the next six months or so and they appeared together in the early 1920 production of *Peter Ibbetson*, as well as other productions. Gradually – and given their profession, perhaps inevitably – their paths began to move in different directions, and they began to see less of each other until parting became a mere formality.

Rathbone wrote, 'The theatre is a hard life for lovers, and harder still for those who would make a successful marriage. "Absence makes the heart grow fonder?" I don't think so.'

Though his romance with Joyce had effectively ended, Basil's career was about to really take off, with the first night of *Peter Ibbetson* being a triumph.

He reflected:

> The opening was a great success and in one night I was launched from obscurity into the limelight of unlimited adulation. Sir Johnstone Forbes Robertson and Sir John Hare came backstage to congratulate me – also Sir Gerald Du Maurier, whose father had written the original story of Peter Ibbetson. Society, titles, statesmen, authors, and actors presented themselves at my dressing room. For the moment, I was the toast of the town.

Indeed, it was exactly the shot in the arm the now 28-year-old actor desperately needed. He had already seen much drama in his life, fleeing South Africa as a child, triumphing at Repton, a father and husband at a relatively young age, war hero and now acclaimed actor. Acting was his passion and, just as it seemed in most things he turned his hand to, he was rather good at it. It was, of course, his true calling, as he had always known it to be.

Regarded as one of the theatre's brightest upcoming talents, doors began to open for Rathbone, who was regularly invited to some of the most exclusive parties in London. At one of them, hosted by the renowned actor and composer Ivor Novello (himself just a year younger than Basil), Anthony Eden, classical actor Henry Ainley and comic actor George Grossmith Junior – among many others – he met his latest love, and for a moment was taken back to his time on the farm in war-torn France.

Though her identity remains a mystery, Basil referred to the mystery woman only as 'Kitten', due to her habit of purring! The affair began at the party after he mistook her for his long-lost *objet de désir*, Marie, who had disappeared after a German bombing raid on her home during the war. He was initially convinced it actually was Marie, and in many ways he was able to live out the fantasy that he was at last in the arms of the woman he had lusted after, if only from a distance.

The pair chatted and laughed before leaving the party and strolling through the streets of London in the early hours of the morning, stopping for an egg and bacon breakfast at a taxicab nightstand before returning to Kitten's apartment. The two were immediately inseparable. His next high-profile role was Iago in *Othello* and again, he received rave reviews for his performance, with the opening night attended by Lloyd George, Lord Balfour, Anthony Eden and Lady Colefax – who later threw a party that he and Kitten attended.

Kitten was distant with Basil throughout the party, and in the taxi on the way home he asked what was wrong. In short, his performance had been so compelling that she was afraid that the devious, calculating character he had played with such conviction could only be carried off by somebody who found such behaviour came easily. He laughed at the suggestion, believing it to be the best review he'd ever had, but Kitten was serious.

'How can you play a part like that and it not be part of you?' she asked, 'You frighten me.' It was not the first time a convincing performance from an actor had led to such suggestions and it wouldn't be the last. Was Basil able to draw from imagined feelings that came easily to him, or was there more to it? Things were never the same between Kitten and Basil after the exchange, and though their passionate affair had burned brightly for more than a year, it was the beginning of the end of their relationship, which would continue for a few months before fizzling out completely. It was his first relationship to suffer for his art.

The plays, leading roles and rave reviews continued throughout 1921. He played Dr Lawson alongside Doris Lloyd in *The Edge O'Beyond* for 150 performances at the Garrick Theatre, and in November he played Tot in *The Painted Laugh* for just a handful of performances, again at the Garrick. It would prove to be his last performance in London for almost a year.

The world of motion pictures was gathering pace in Europe and the United States, and the next logical step for Basil was to make his movie debut – this he did in the 1921 British silent film *Innocent*. Basil plays the ruthless Amadis de Jocelyn – an early indicator of what lay ahead for him – and though his portrayal of a seducing artist won praise, the film, shot at Cricklewood Studios, was average at best. He would quickly follow *Innocent* with *The Fruitful Vine*, another silent movie filmed at Cricklewood and another movie that has been long forgotten in the annals of time.

While neither picture would propel him to instant fame and fortune, they were part of his apprenticeship and added to his body of work. Silent movies, of course, denied the audience one of Basil's most powerful tools – his voice – though there would be many more opportunities in the future.

Basil's next adventure would change his life forever, after he won a part in *The Czarina* at New York City's Empire Theatre on Broadway.

It would be start of a lifelong love of America and feed Basil's hunger for new horizons and adventure completely. On 21 December 1921, he set sail from Southampton on the SS *Olympic*, bound for New York.

His first sight of the Manhattan skyline as the ship approached its destination left a sizeable impression on him, as he recalled:

After spending Christmas Day at sea, in the early hours of the following morning the New York skyline rose majestically with the dawn, like a portrait by Arthur Rackham. I was emotionally stunned by its beauty and every time since I have left or returned to New York by sea, I have had the same reaction.

Of course, he would return home many times in the years that followed, but his future now lay on the other side of the Atlantic Ocean where the 'land of opportunities' would prove irresistible to the 29-year-old Rathbone. Though he won praise for his portrayal of Count Alexei Czerny, the play, which had brief spells in Washington and Baltimore, was only a moderate success and not quite the vehicle that would launch his career Stateside. Unbeknown to Basil, a woman who was watching his performance in *The Czarina* turned to her friend during the play and said: 'One day, I'm going to marry that man.'

It wouldn't happen immediately, but Ouida Bergere would eventually get her man.

6

1922–1925

An Englishman in New York

The fact is: It's true what they say about the United States. It is a land of opportunity. It is too various to get bored with it.

Christopher Hitchens

Little is known of the time Basil spent between *The Czarina* and his next job, which was several weeks away, but it is likely he took the opportunity to see some of America while he had the time to explore. One such jaunt to Cape Cod saw him stay at The Red Inn in Provincetown for the night, though who his guest was remains a mystery. He signed in the guest register on 27 June 1922 as 'Mr. and Mrs. Basil Rathbone, London, England' – as Marion and he were separated, it is almost certain that the mystery woman was not his wife and more likely a woman he'd met along the way and had a romantic break with.

Basil found time to return to Britain to film his third picture, though his role in the silent movie *The Loves of Mary, Queen of Scots*, filmed in Scotland, was uncredited and likely took up little of his time. 'It was perhaps an easy job for good pay' more than anything else and a chance to further expand his experience and body of work for future gain.

It had been the renowned theatre producer Gilbert Miller who had signed Basil up for his first Broadway production in *The Czarina* and, now under contract, it was Miller who sanctioned his return to London to appear in Somerset Maugham's *East of Suez* at Her Majesty's Theatre. He then appeared in a lengthy run of *R.U.R* at St Martin's Theatre, London. He had spent almost a year back in the capital before returning to the States, where he evidently felt his future lay. A hopeless romantic and a born adventurer, America and all its openings and optimism remained the perfect destination for Rathbone. He was intoxicated by the verve and energy of New York and he had no plans to return to London any time soon.

He appeared briefly in *The Next Corner* at New York's Plymouth Theatre before landing the role of Dr Nicholas Agi in *The Swan* – the play where everything changed for Basil.

He recalled:

In the fall of 1923 Gilbert Miller brought me back to America. *The Swan* by Ferenc Molnar is probably the most memorable play of my life. I loved it passionately – and it made me a star in America. *The Swan*, with Eva Le Gallienne, Phillip Merrivale, and myself was a dismal failure in its try-out weeks in Detroit and Toronto. Gilbert was all for closing the play in Toronto. However, fate ruled otherwise, and we opened at the Cort Theatre in New York on October 23, 1923. The day had been heavy with moisture and as curtain time approached a veritable cloudburst poured from the heavens. We played the first act to a house that slowly filled up, having struggled to get to the theatre, and which was mostly in understandably bad humour. At the end of the first act we received a mild reception. Going back to our dressing rooms, Philip Merrivale said, 'Well, I guess Gilbert was right, we're a flop.' The second act, however, went well, and at the final curtain we received a standing ovation. I saw a man about fourth row centre throw his hat in the air. I learned later that it was Alexander Woollcott. The next day we had a matinee, and there was a queue at the box office a block long – we were a tremendous success.

The Swan was indeed something of a phenomenon. It proved to be Basil's first major success on Broadway, running for 528 performances all told and firmly establishing him as a Broadway star and enhancing his growing reputation.

He relished the role, made it his own and reaped the rewards. All his efforts since the war were finally bearing fruit and his determination to make something happen had been fully vindicated.

As word spread of this dashing English actor who was taking Broadway by storm, so the media became interested in finding out more about him. The 23 November (1923) issue of *Billboard* ran a feature that gave a taste of just how quickly Basil's star was rising.

It read:

When our dramatic critic, in his review of 'The Swan' defined Mr Basil Rathbone as 'the leading man par excellence with the looks, bearing and acting capacity which should go with the genius' we decided that we had a clue worth following in our search for interesting personalities. But getting a seat for a performance of 'The Swan' was like getting poor Humpty up again. It was only due to the cancellation of a third balcony box reservation that we succeeded in viewing that ideal couple, the fair Eva La Gallienne and the stalwart Rathbone. We gazed so long from our dizzy heights thru the lenses of an opera glass that we became dizzy and were obliged to seek the wings backstage for a close up of Mr Rathbone.

We found him surrounded by a bevy of femininity and reporters. Closing our eyes to everyone's claim of prior presence we began harping on Mr Rathbone's name in varying keys until one of them registered in that gentleman's ear. He bowed deeply to signify that his attention was ours, but he submitted to an interview about as gracefully as a caged Bengal tiger, gliding hither and thither until we would have given our meagre kingdom for a pair of roller skates that would have enabled our five feet five to keep pace with the long sweeping six feet plus Rathbone glides.

Though he demurred an interview that evening, he promised to deliver his thoughts on paper the following day. He didn't – instead, he turned up at *Billboard*'s offices to give his opinions on all manner of subjects, with his love of America and its people immediately evident.

Rathbone told the reporter:

> There, that is what I think of America – hurry, hurry, hurry! Wonderful city, instinct with vitality! It vitalizes me, too. If I had my way I should tour back and forth across America, gathering vitality from New York, ozone in the majestic Rockies, inspiration from the great desert, and California, gosh how I love California! I'd settle down in California to rest, if I could rest. But I could never be faithful to one place long. My temperament is too restless. I believe constant change is as necessary to the person of imagination as colour and form variety are to nature and art. To rest means to rust – mentally.

He continued:

> The theatre in America is as much of an institution as the railroads. It is necessary to your people's progress as existence, for they love it. They don't go to the theatre in quest of relaxation as so many aver, but because they love it and because it stimulates them. It's the great panacea that keeps your men from becoming mere working automatons!

The article concluded:

> How brilliant this young English actor is! And how handsome! He reminds one of Lou Tellergen in a way – the same classic head and profile, made more dominant and vital by a darkness of colouring suggesting Norman ancestry.

The Swan's success was the break and exposure he had desperately needed in the States and his life would never be quite the same again. Nor would his personal life.

Though he had been dating a woman called June, Basil was clearly looking for something with more depth and longevity, and in November 1923 he met the woman he would spend the rest of his life with.

Ouida Bergere was a complicated character and one of New York's leading socialites. Even before she met her husband-to-be, she was known for her lavish parties for A-listers and prominent members of society. Though she had predicted she would one day marry Basil after watching him on Broadway, their paths hadn't crossed since, until, by chance, he was invited to one of Ouida's parties.

He recalled:

> Late in November 1923, I met Clifton Webb on the street, and he asked if I'd like to go to a party after the play. I asked whose party and he said: 'Ouida Bergere, she's divine … you'll love her. She's a darling … come on, everyone will be there, and Ouida won't mind. Besides, it'll be like Grand Central Station anyway and you'll be lucky if you meet her.

Intrigued, Basil asked if he could bring June and then agreed to attend later that evening.

He was immediately impressed by Ouida's first-floor apartment at 53rd and Madison, set within what he described as a 'lovely old building' that would later be taken over by CBS Studios.

Basil and June settled down in a corner while Clifton went in search of Ouida to introduce them, but she was, by all accounts, having supper with the Italian ambassador in another room. June knew of Ouida, who was Paramount's leading scriptwriter at the time and a woman with obvious power and social standing. She described her as 'young, petite, strongly opinionated and very successful' – Basil's recollection that June was perhaps jealous or concerned about Ouida was clear when he added that the description had 'a touch of vinegar' about it. No wonder! Not long after, Ouida made a dramatic entrance to the room and Basil was enraptured immediately.

He recalled:

> Somewhere, there was a hustle and bustle as a door opened and Ouida and her friends re-joined the party. We were introduced and she kissed June. She was indeed young and petite; with the most beautiful natural red hair I have ever seen… eyes that danced with the joy of living and skin texture like alabaster. She wore a yellow, low-cut evening dress that flared at the waist. She was the prefect Renoir. A moment later, she was gone, but not before smiling sweetly and saying: 'You will enjoy yourselves, won't you?'

Basil was certain she remembered him from *The Czarina*, along with the pledge she'd made to her friend at the time as she watched on. Two days later, Ouida invited Basil, June and several mutual acquaintances to stay with her at her home at Great Neck, Long Island. June, one would imagine, must have had her suspicions that Basil had been quite taken with Ouida, and perhaps even ventured to Long Island with a sense of foreboding. Her intuition was accurate. The beginning of the end of her relationship with Basil had started at the moment he'd met Ouida and been hopelessly smitten by her. It wasn't the first time in his life he had fallen in love at first sight, and as her Rolls Royce drove them from the train station to her impressive home on the Sound, Basil must have felt destiny was also guiding him towards a future that had always been meant to be.

The pair began dating shortly after, with poor June cast aside in the fallout. She wasn't the first woman in his life to be cast aside, but the chemistry between Basil and Ouida had been obvious and left a certain inevitability about proceedings. There was something different about Ouida and Basil. Destiny, it seems, was most definitely playing its hand – or had Ouida carefully engineered the whole situation? Basil was legally still married and had a young son back in England whom he rarely saw.

Years after, Basil's granddaughter Dounia Rathbone revealed:

> What I know of Marion after Basil left is that she was angry
> and upset that he did what he did and felt pretty abandoned,
> which it seems she was. She was left with a very young son
> whom Basil wanted nothing to do with. She continued to be
> an amazing Shakespearean actor with the Benson Company
> despite everything.

And there was another complication in his love life – Basil's co-star
in *The Swan* was the beautiful London-born actress Eva Le Gallienne,
who was 25 years old when they first met.

Le Gallienne was playing Alexandra and her biographer, Helen
Sheehy, who wrote *Eva Le Gallienne: A Biography* in 1996, quoted
Eva saying how much she enjoyed working with Rathbone:

> Better than any man I have ever played with. He is entirely charm-
> ing – very gentle and nice to me – and wonderful to play with (he
> is the first leading man I have ever had who is earnest and deeply
> sincere about his work – who never cheats or in any way shirks his
> end of things). He likes me too – and we both hope we may do
> many things together in the future.

Over time, and when *The Swan* went on tour in the autumn
of 1924 – and despite Le Gallienne's long-term relationship with
another woman – she began a relationship with Basil, almost certainly after he and Ouida had become an item.

Sheehy claims that Eva 'was attracted to Rathbone on every level –
sexually, artistically, and spiritually. She adored his "long aristocratic
legs," his gentle nature, and they were both schooled in European and
English theatre, loved the classics and shared artistic aspirations.'

It is even suggested that, at one point, Le Gallienne told her
long-time partner, Mercedes de Acosta, that she thought of marrying Basil and having his child. It seems this unusual affair continued
during the lengthy tour *The Swan* embarked on across America,

and probably lasted until the spring of 1925 when conflicting reports surfaced that one or the other ended the relationship. Despite this, Eva clearly retained feelings for Basil. She later wrote to her mother, 'I still call him "my" Basil, because I know that he really is. I miss him.'

It seems unlikely that Ouida knew of the affair. She may have suspected it, or she might have had no knowledge – most likely the latter, given that Le Gallienne's sexual preferences were common knowledge in the theatre world.

Either way, it was Ouida who would win the day, with Basil needing a more settled personal life at such a crucial stage of his career. He had already seen so much, experienced and lived enough for two lifetimes and, aged 31, he was now approaching a new level of stardom. His restless, adventurous spirit was calmed by Ouida, who was five years his senior – just as Marion had been – and despite his affair with Eva, his marriage to Ouida had become an inevitability.

However, there were still some loose ends to tie up before he could officially make Ouida Mrs Rathbone No. 2 …

7

1925–1926

Hollywood Beckons

Hollywood is a place where they'll pay you a thousand dollars
for a kiss and fifty cents for your soul.

Marilyn Monroe

Basil and Ouida made a decision early in their relationship that made
sense to each of them, but would, in time, pile enormous pressure
onto Basil's shoulders. Ouida was reportedly earning $1,500 per week
as scriptwriter – $20,000 in today's money – while Basil was earn-
ing $500 per week (approximately $6,500 today) from his Broadway
work, but with the ambition burning fiercely in Basil's soul and his
prospects in the industry seemingly limitless, it was Ouida who asked
to be released from her contract with Paramount. This would allow
her to be with her fiancé as often as she wanted and help manage
his career, rather than having to spend long periods on projects on
the West Coast. Both had experienced relationships where work and
enforced separation put tremendous strain on one or both partners
and ultimately ended with a parting of the ways. They were in love
and neither wanted to be apart from the other, so the arrangement
was perhaps the only way forward.

Ouida was no fool, either. She knew Basil's star was rising rapidly and the likelihood was he would soon be earning more than enough to keep her in the lifestyle she had become accustomed to, while Basil was the first to admit he led a fairly 'monastic' existence, happy if he had a bed to sleep in, clothes on his back and food in his stomach. He was perhaps one of the least materialistic men in showbusiness at that time.

Basil wrote of the reaction to Ouida's decision:

> This may, in retrospect, sound like good sense, but it also required a courage and devotion that many of Ouida's friends considered to be considerably 'beyond the call of duty!' Samuel Goldwyn was disgusted with Ouida's decision and promised to buy her a grand piano if she would give up the idea of marrying 'this actor!' Jack Miltern, who knew of and had experienced Ouida's extravagance, was heartily opposed to our union, and I am sure there were many others who knew us both and who could do no more than wish us a happy if somewhat limited 'fling!'

It would be anything but a fling.

The Swan, meanwhile, had become something of a phenomenon. An exhaustive thirteen-month tour of the US, playing to packed houses in Chicago, Milwaukee, St Louis, Brooklyn, Washington, Philadelphia, Newark, Riviera (New Jersey), Boston, New Haven, Albany, Cleveland and Pittsburgh took its toll on the cast.

During the tour, Basil also appeared in his first US silent movie, the 1924 production of *Trouping with Ellen*, playing a sizeable role in the film. *Variety* magazine reported that the lead character's rival was 'well played by Basil Rathbone'. It was another small, but vital, step in the right direction.

The summer of 1924 would also see Basil return to England to try and convince his wife Marion to grant him a divorce – something she had until then steadfastly refused to do, perhaps hopeful that there might one day be a reconciliation between them. Divorce was the last, inevitable phase of a marriage that had effectively ended many years before, but in order to marry Ouida, there was a legal necessity to make everything official between Basil and his wife of ten years. Later, in a published magazine interview in *True Story*, he explained: 'I came from an old-school family which did not believe in divorce ... When a Rathbone married, he stayed married, regardless of the circumstances. They had barely forgiven me for taking up acting as a profession. I knew all too well what their reaction to a divorce would be.' But eventually, and perhaps seeing the futility of the situation, Marion finally agreed to a legal separation.

Ouida and Jack Miltern, a close friend of Ouida's and twenty-three years Basil's senior, travelled to England where Ouida had found a beautiful house on the River Thames to rent for the summer. *The Swan* had paused for a summer break so there were no immediate work commitments and Basil finally had the chance to recharge his batteries. It was a glorious English summer and a reminder for Basil that, while his heart was now in America, he still loved to come home every now and then. Ouida and Basil enjoyed many long walks or punted down the Thames to a local pub in their idyllic location in Pangbourne, Berkshire – some 60 miles from the centre of London.

Basil saw friends and family and tied up several loose ends, but seeing his father was not on his itinerary, as he had sadly passed away aged 68 on 13 June – Basil's 32nd birthday – and a few weeks before he travelled home for the summer.

In his autobiography, he recalled the trip and clearly took comfort from the manner of his father's passing:

I was determined that Ouida and I should be free to marry as soon as possible, and to do so I needed both legal advice and the opportunity to convince Marion that our long separation should now be legally terminated. This visit home had another and less happy purpose. My dear father had died on my birthday, June thirteenth. He had been very ill but was well on the way to recovery, and was recuperating in the country with his sister, my Aunt Ethel. 'Daddie' died as he had lived, in circumstances that I think deserve the term dramatic. It was a beautiful early summer morning and he was seated comfortably before his bedroom window, looking out into a rose garden that was freshly in bloom. Aunt Ethel brought him his breakfast tray and a letter from me. She had paused while he opened my letter and read it to her. It had made him very happy.

About half an hour later Aunt Ethel had returned to his room to collect his breakfast tray. His breakfast remained untouched and he appeared to be sleeping peacefully, my letter still in his hand. He was dead. I like to think that my mother was somewhere close by to meet him. It would have been good to have had Ouida know my father, who would have loved her so much. She would have been just his 'cup of tea' … God bless him.

Basil had now lost both his parents and his divorce was settled, but during the trip there had been no mention of his then 8-year-old son, Rodion, something that would rankle his descendants in the years to come. After a six-week stay in England, Basil sailed back to Boston ahead of *The Swan*'s September reopening at the Empire in New York, and the play would also take up most of the following year, ending with an eight-week run in San Francisco from April until the end of May 1925.

That year, Basil also appeared in his fifth silent movie, *The Masked Bride*, again receiving favourable reviews; but again, this wouldn't be the film that propelled him to a national audience. It had, however, been his first Hollywood movie and further endorsed his initial love of California. He returned to New York after several weeks filming and appeared in several stage productions in and around his adopted city and also in Massachusetts, while Ouida made plans for an inevitably lavish wedding ceremony.

Her Christmas present to Basil in 1925 was a story in itself, as they rescued a German Shepherd from a near-certain death sentence. They met the actor George Revenant, a friend, in his dressing room after a show, and he introduced them to his dog, Moritz, who was an obedient 3-year-old former police dog, and explained that his faithful companion had killed a sheep and he had to appear in court in a few days' time where the verdict would almost certainly see the dog destroyed. Ouida quickly concocted a story to not only ensure Moritz escaped death, but that he would have a new home and new life with them in Manhattan. They paid George $200 and it was decided there and then that Moritz would be spirited away under the premise that he had been stolen. George agreed – he couldn't bear the thought of his dog being put to sleep in the prime of his life and he knew he would likely have a wonderful life with Basil and Ouida. It would be the start of Basil's love of dogs, and he would surround himself with them through much of his life in America.

After leaving for Philadelphia, Moritz was hidden in the hotel room that Basil had booked for a couple of weeks – a lesser-known, non-showbusiness establishment called The Sylvania – while Ouida stayed at The Ritz. The plan worked perfectly. Moritz was obedient and went to work with Basil each evening, sleeping in his dressing room until his performance had ended, and then was spirited back to the hotel under the cover of darkness. While it's unlikely Moritz had been the subject of a FBI all-points bulletin, just one paparazzi photograph with Basil could have signed his death warrant. With the dust settled, Moritz eventually returned to New York with the couple and, despite only understanding German commands to begin with, became inseparable from Basil who would rarely be seen without the dog from then on. Ouida's scriptwriting skills were clearly still sharp, with Moritz's true identity never surfacing during the next eleven years that he was at Basil's side. As a footnote, the court accepted George's story that his dog had been stolen, and the matter was closed.

Meanwhile, Ouida had cleared a path to marrying Basil. On 18 June 1925, the *New York Review* reported, 'Basil Rathbone, leading man for Elsie Ferguson at the Biltmore Theatre, has admitted his engagement to Ouida Bergere, former wife of George Fitzmaurice, the picture director. Fitzmaurice was awarded a divorce from his wife here in December on the grounds of desertion.'

Years later, Basil would write that he was unsure how Ouida would feel about divorcing her husband, saying: 'I knew that she was separated from her husband, but I did not know how she felt about divorce.' The truth was Ouida was very comfortable with divorce, having been through the process twice before! She had already been Mrs Burgess and Mrs Weadock in her earlier marriages but there was no mention of this in Basil's autobiography, indicating the possibility that he wasn't even aware that he would be her fourth husband – was it possible that Basil didn't know about Ouida's earlier marriages? There was, perhaps, good reason he didn't particularly want the wider world to know, as a three-times divorcee would surely have set the gossip columnists and showbiz writers' tongues wagging.

After a two-year courtship, Basil, 34, and Ouida, 39, were married on 18 April 1926. Both being divorcees, it proved difficult to find a church for the marriage to take place and in the end, their wedding took place at their friend Joseph Thomas's apartment in Manhattan with Father Hampden of the Dutch Reformed Church presiding.

The *Movie Mirror* reported:

> Basil's best friend had kindly lent a luxurious Park Avenue apartment, and, high above the milling crowds, the magnificent, top-floor suite had been transformed into an exquisite setting. One room had been specially built into a little chapel, and before a flower-drenched altar, with acolytes swinging incense, Basil had exchanged rings with his bride. A chosen dozen had been invited for the ceremony proper, but afterwards three hundred distinguished guests had thronged the apartment for the gay reception.

The following day, Basil joined the filming of his final silent movie, a $250,000 budget (about $4 million in today's money) picture called *The Great Deception* in New York, and would spend the next few months playing a German agent called Rizzio.

The movie did well at the box office and again brought Basil Rathbone to a wider American audience, but it would prove to be just the tip of the iceberg, with greater successes just around the corner. But one fact that would come to light shortly after their marriage is at odds with Ouida's image of being a wealthy woman. She was anything but. While it is true she was working for a major studio prior to meeting Basil, it seems much of her supposed wealth may have been cleverly exaggerated. She was clearly a woman of expensive tastes and she certainly enjoyed the high life and mixing with high society, but was she in fact writing cheques her bank account couldn't sustain? The swanky Long Island home, the expensive car, clothes and parties all cost a small fortune. If she had plenty of money none of this would have proved a huge issue (although it perhaps was not sustainable indefinitely), and it certainly kept her firmly in the eye of high society.

Could she even have been rolling the dice as she looked for husband number four? While her decision to stop working and be by Basil's side and focus on his career certainly has a touch of nobility about it, in today's money, she would have been earning a healthy $80,000 per month. It was a vast amount to toss away casually, it would appear. And if her belief that a woman's place was by her man was so steadfast, it does beg the question as to why she hadn't stopped working when married to her previous husband, George Fitzmaurice?

And why, just eight weeks after becoming Mrs Basil Rathbone, did Ouida file for bankruptcy? A notice published in the *New York Times* detailed that Ouida had personal assets of just $150 and liabilities of $9,399 – approximately $150,000 in today's money. Something didn't add up, and it wasn't only Ouida's bank account.

8

1926–1929

Lights, Camera, Action!

We have really everything in common with America nowadays except, of course, language.

Oscar Wilde

Basil continued to appear in many successful Broadway plays as the 1920s progressed. His reputation continued to grow while his seemingly idyllic marriage to Ouida was proving the rock his personal life had needed.

They summered in Maine – along with the ever-faithful Moritz, of course – and often Ouida's close friend Jack Miltern would stay with them. Jack had become a friend of Basil, who considered him to be something of a second father.

There is little doubt that Ouida's decision to allow her career to take a back seat had been a wise one and the couple were blissfully happy. To move Basil's career on to the next level, he needed a box office success that would elevate him from meaty supporting roles to being the leading man in pictures. He was desperate for a vehicle that could bring all his talents together for the audiences, and in 1929 he won the part that would change everything for him.

Hollywood was desperate to churn out talking pictures and studios sent talent scouts to Broadway, which was obviously a veritable hotbed of acting talent. Many shows were stripped of their stars, who accepted the lucrative financial carrots to sign up for movie deals as the Hollywood talent drain began in earnest.

Basil would join the exodus but wasn't entirely comfortable with the situation.

He opined:

> When the silent picture became a talking picture, it lost its original art form and became a derivative of the theatre. It exploded all over the world, and a gigantic migration took place to the West Coast, where millions upon millions of dollars were invested, real estate boomed, enormous concrete soundproof stages rose like mushrooms overnight – directors, writers, actors, musicians, and technicians were at a premium, and Broadway was invaded by an army of salesmen with unlimited spending accounts. Slowly but surely the original magic was being mislaid – except for a few 'dreamers' who remembered where the magic was hidden.

After agreeing a short-term contract with MGM in February 1929 (with an option to extend), filming began on his first 'talkie' – and one that earned Basil a sizeable pay cheque, given that Ouida had torn up the original contract and gone to MGM's New York representative where she managed to double her husband's salary! Sharp business acumen was needed at the time and Ouida clearly knew the game studios played.

The Last of Mrs Cheyney proved to be a huge success and, at last, people could hear his classic, commanding yet eloquent British voice and were duly captivated. It was the final piece of his career jigsaw, with Basil's unique voice a huge asset on the silver screen.

The all-important review in the *New York Times* reported Rathbone's performance to be 'capital' and added that his poise and conduct were perfect for the role of the wealthy playboy Lord Dilling.

The co-star Norma Shearer and her real-life husband – producer Irving Thalberg – were close friends with Basil and Ouida and had undoubtedly held some sway in the casting. Indeed, Basil commented later:

> In all the years we have known her, Norma Shearer has never changed one iota. Her charm and warm friendship and classic beauty are as gracious and warm and classic today as on the first day we met her. If she and I had not both been so happily married, I am quite sure I would have fallen very much in love with her!

Given Basil's past loves, there was more than a grain of truth in that observation. *The Last of Mrs Cheyney* was only MGM's second talking picture. Directed by Sydney Franklin, it made Basil not quite the overnight star, but a leading man of huge promise. Franklin said:

> Basil Rathbone was a great help to [Norma] in that picture; I remember that she went out of her way to ask him to discuss without hesitancy anything he felt was out of key in her performance or her inflections, vocally, and he took her at her word, and she was happy to get whatever advice he chose to impart. Basil got very impatient with the mikes hidden in flowerpots and the stationary camera in its lined case that stood stock still and prevented him from roaming around the soundstage as he did in the theatre. So, they sort of consoled each other – that first year of sound was rough on actors – and directors.

The doors of Hollywood had well and truly swung open, with the thirst for talking pictures ensuring that Basil's slate was quickly filled as demand for him to play the lead in several pictures planned for 1930 release grew. His experiences and hard work on Broadway and in a number of silent films had served him well, but there was little doubt, in turn, that he had now served his apprenticeship and could begin to enjoy the fruits of his labour (which had been considerable).

The offers flooded in, and with Ouida's connections and eye for a great script, it was a magical time for the Rathbones.

His next movie – *The Bishop Murder Case* – could easily have served as an early audition for Sherlock Holmes, with many striking similarities to The Great Detective. He takes the lead as 'gentleman detective' Philo Vance and is invited by his friend, District Attorney Markham, to help solve a murder. Vance, a 'cultured eccentric', uses cunning and craft in his observations, and when a suspect is arrested he is far from convinced, stating, 'This is no ordinary crime. And we cannot proceed in an ordinary manner. Mark my words: this is not a single murder we are trying to solve; it is the beginning of a series of murders, ghastly and inhuman.'

It was dialogue that could easily have been delivered by Holmes himself.

In the film, actor Roland Young even refers to Vance as Sherlock Holmes – it was an odd coincidence, given what lay in store some nine years down the line for Rathbone, or was it the hand of fate that had so often played a part in his life?

Basil's MGM contract was extended and he and Ouida travelled from Long Island to Hollywood for each new project, with Ouida in her element, attending dinners, parties and weddings, networking with the studio executives and influencers of the day. With six more movies to make in 1930, it quickly became evident that the Rathbones needed to have a permanent residence in California, and so in April they moved into their new home at 628 Crescent Drive, Beverly Hills, with Ouida organising a lavish housewarming – just four days after they arrived.

While Ouida entertained, Basil continued to carve his career in Hollywood, appearing in *A Notorious Affair*, *A Lady Surrenders*, *The Lady of Scandal*, *This Mad World*, *The Flirting Widow* and *Sin Takes a Holiday*.

The workload, the endless parties and functions, must have tired a man who was used to a simpler existence, and the fact that *The Film Daily* reported Basil was to return to New York to seek a stage job perhaps indicates he was not entirely happy with his lot – or at least needed to touch base with his first love, the theatre, and maintain his sanity.

In effect, after *Sin Takes a Holiday*, Basil took a holiday – from the silver screen at least – and wouldn't make another film for two years. He agreed to appear in *A Woman Commands*, slated for a 1932 release, but in between he appeared in a number of Broadway productions, beginning with *A Kiss of Importance* at the Fulton Theatre, which ran for twenty-four performances. He then took the lead in the February 1931 production of *Heatwave*, again at the Fulton Theatre and another short-term stint with the play lasting fifteen performances, while the April production of *Melo* – at the Ethel Barrymore Theatre in New York – ran for sixty-seven performances.

In the autumn, Basil returned to Hollywood to film *A Woman Commands* (Ouida would have no doubt approved!) but was back in New York by the first week of November where rehearsals for *The Devil Passes* would soon begin. The play opened for a week in Philadelphia in late December 1931, and would stay for a week at the Broad Street Theatre before opening on Broadway, where it proved a sizeable success, running for just shy of 100 performances before going on an extensive tour of major US cities.

Basil broke off as and when needed to fulfil his movie commitments and attended the premiere of *A Woman Commands* at the Mayfair in New York.

The movie's budget was just shy of $500,000, but it grossed less than half that sum and was a surprising hiccup for the seemingly relentless rise of Basil Rathbone. But as he once stated, working in the movies was not like the theatre – you got paid handsomely whether the film made a profit or suffered substantial losses. That was at least one upside of the movie business.

He is believed to have been preparing for his next MGM movie in May 1932 – *Reunion in Vienna* – but after receiving a better offer in England, he decided to return home for a spell. He was desperately homesick, despite his obvious love of the States, and perhaps needed a complete break from the showbiz parties, galas and premieres to realign his focus.

The reception he would receive when he returned to England as a rising Hollywood star would both surprise and disappoint him …

9

1930–1933

England, my England?

Look not mournfully into the past, it comes not back again.
Wisely improve the present, it is thine. Go forth to meet the
shadowy future without fear and with a manly heart.

Henry Wadsworth Longfellow

They say you should never go back. In Basil Rathbone's case, this was
probably true. He had – for now – turned his back on Hollywood
and instead pursued a movie career back in England. He had clearly
been missing home and had tired of the movie star life in California.
He was a performer and an artist, yet he felt like neither as he churned
out film after film in Tinseltown.

Going home seemed the perfect panacea, and though initially he
detected something close to a frosty reception on his return, he was
determined to help the British film industry not only compete with
Hollywood, but perhaps take the lead. More than ever, it seemed he
had become jaundiced with his life in America and needed an escape
from what he saw as increasingly phoney existence.

He wrote:

I was very homesick for my motherland, and Ouida, who has always been most patient with me in these moods, encouraged me to return to the London theatre. But, to my surprise, I was received in London with a sort of 'Oh, you're back again are you?' attitude, as though I were doing something unethical! I had been away too long and my Broadway successes in *The Swan*, *The Captive*, and *The Command to Love* did not have the effect I had anticipated they would. This visit home was made worthwhile professionally by a motion picture I made of Galsworthy's play *Loyalties* in which I played de Levis, the Jew, under the direction of Mr Basil Dean. This picture and my performance in it received considerable commendation, and I shall always consider it to be one of my most fortunate experiences.

During his return, he stayed with Ouida at a guest house in Penn, Buckinghamshire, and it was there that he finally saw his classically handsome son, Rodion – by now aged 17 – and they got to know each other again. Basil and Rodion had been writing to each other frequently in recent years, though Basil spoke little of his son either publicly or later in his autobiography. There was a suspicion that Ouida had organised the reunion, but this was vehemently denied by Rodion's family in later years who claimed exactly the opposite, that Ouida had worked hard to keep father and son apart. The truth will likely never be known.

Basil had been home four months when he received an offer from renowned actress, theatre owner, writer and producer Katherine Cornell, dubbed 'the first lady of theatre', to tour the US with a production of *Romeo and Juliet*, *The Barretts of Wimpole Street* and *Candida*. It was an intriguing offer with three fascinating roles on offer for Basil who, it seemed, could never resist his favourite role as Romeo. Both he and Ouida travelled to Bavaria to meet her and discuss the project. The meeting went well and he agreed that he would join the tour, with rehearsals to begin immediately.

Basil's frank interview in the January 1933 edition of *Picturegoer* showed his resentment for Hollywood at that time was never far from the surface. Between filming of *After the Ball* – his first British talkie – he was keen to get one or two things off his chest, it seemed. Interviewed by *Picturegoer*'s Helen Trevelyan, Basil believed British filmmakers were every bit as talented as their American cousins, but they could ill-afford to fall too far behind Hollywood.

'This is the hour of our opportunity,' he said:

There is hardly a British star previously lost to this country, whom we could not buy back if we chose, today. We have the equipment, the material, and the brains. This is the hour of our opportunity.

It depends entirely on our producers. Actors, actresses, and scenario writers are powerless without initiative and foresight from the producer, who, after all, has the whole say in how things shall be done.

With him lies the destiny of the British picture. And, moreover, in eighteen months if we have not made good, we never shall. This is our big moment and we must win through.

I have great faith in our ability to pull it off, otherwise I should not have deliberately walked out on *Reunion in Vienna*, which I was to have played in California with Ina Claire and come back here. I believe that we can not only equal, but rival any and every other country's films; but will we?

It seemed the Broadway talent drain troubled Rathbone greatly, even though he himself had been part of the whole process. At least at the time, it seemed to have left a bad taste in his mouth:

There are two very grave dangers which threaten our success. One is the fatal habit of drawing upon actors from the stage to fill screen parts. It can't be done. A man cannot serve two masters; his work is bound to suffer if he tries and he will be responsible sooner or later for letting one or both severely down.

In Hollywood, one is 3,000 miles from the theatre; it is impossible to combine the two, and so it should be over here. They are distinct, separate, and whole-time jobs. Our second danger lies in not having formed the nucleus of stock companies. For we must make stars. People do not go to films only to see pictures; they go to see stars.

It is not the impersonal which attracts them, but the purely personal. It is individualism that counts. Personality! Personality! Personality!

Between artist and director, there must be perfect understanding before ever the story is begun; otherwise there can be no harmony anywhere on the set. They must both know beforehand how they intend the part to be played, and then the director will convey to the actor the impression he wishes to get from him, and the actor will respond through his own peculiar personality.

Thus, six stars might be given the same scene to enact, and each would approach it from an entirely different angle, while still satisfying the director's instruction. That is what is known as co-operation, and it is vitally important between producer and player.

How do I learn my lines? I learn the whole play – yes, every-body's parts! – as soon as it is given me and allow it all to soak thoroughly well into my system before I am called upon to deliver it. So that when the time does come, I am not bothered for words, but can give myself up to the complicated mechanism of film acting.

No, I'm afraid I have no use for actors who profess 'to lose them-selves' in their parts. How can they, when all the while one has to be so painfully conscious that it is with the left hand one does this, and on the right foot?

To be unaware of camera, lights, and spacing would be to act right out of the photographer's range! And too, really to lose your-self would mean being genuinely in love with every actress to whom you made love – and that would be very exhausting!

Besides, there is no continuity to a film actor's part. It is a series of bits, all chopped about and changed, and finally stuck together. A tremendous aid in building a star's popularity hitherto denied to the film actor, is, of course, the voice. This is so much more telling, more powerful than the face, and has been responsible for a total re-assortment in the stellar metropolis.

It was an almost cathartic outburst by Basil, who clearly needed to get his thoughts out into the wider world and off his chest. Interestingly, the interviewer asked whether his return home was a fleeting one, and at that point he seemed set on making the move away from California a permanent one.

'Rather not!' he responded emphatically:

I'm home for good, I hope. Whether I shall continue to make pictures here depends on our opening sentence! But I don't want to go back to Hollywood.

It's so unbelievably dull. Less happens there than anywhere else I've ever been. Its parties are as formal as any you could hope to find. All those reports concerning wild affairs have been taken from a few isolated instances and magnified to an impossible degree.

I am perfectly certain that in every large community in the world there are instances of rowdy parties that would make 'copy,' but not as good 'copy' as instances in the film world, because the public wishes for such copy.

Deny your public stories about picture people, and a majority of those picture people would dwindle in popularity very soon. The public romances about the picture world and thank God they do.

It is all good copy, and a legitimate source of income to newspapers and magazines and the industry itself, so why worry about it? Except in a few isolated cases, no one gets hurt and a lot of people make a lot of money out of it!

There is another side of life in the picture world that is, however, little touched on, and that is far more interesting than any other. For one success there are a hundred failures. The majority of those concerned in making pictures are sad, disillusioned people, with unfulfilled dreams and ambitions. Thousands live in this fair land of sunshine and flowers and hopes and promises, and only a very, very few realise anything.

Hollywood is a cruel place – relentless, stern, and unforgiving – as I suppose all great industrial centres must be. But, after all, this industry is trading in human material – very beautiful human material, and very sensitive. The tragedy of Hollywood should be written. Boredom is one's greatest enemy in Hollywood, and a married couple must have the utmost consideration for each other under such circumstances, as only a very strong attachment can stand it.

It was a surprisingly honest account of a life he clearly loathed at that stage, yet those feelings would change. Or would it be Ouida's influence that would convince him to return to America and continue his flourishing career? It seems almost certainly to have been the latter, with Basil clearly determined at that stage to put as much distance between himself and Hollywood as possible. Either way, he completed the movie *Loyalties* – Associated Talking Pictures' first production (they would later become Ealing Studios) – before continuing to rehearse for Katherine Cornell's ambitious three-play tour of the USA in the fall of 1933. He was returning to America, but it was on his terms.

It would turn out to be something of a Second Coming in terms of his career across the Atlantic, but this time, he wanted to do things his own way, with his theatrical life taking precedence.

10

1933–1935

Box Office and Hate Mail

There is a difference between a villain and one who simply commits a crime. The villain is an extremely conscious person and commits a crime consciously, for its own sake.

W.H. Auden

In October 1933, Basil and Ouida returned to the United States, with his schedule about to shift up another gear as a lead player in Katherine Cornell's three-play tour. He would feature in *Romeo and Juliet*, *The Barretts of Wimpole Street* and *Candida*, playing the parts of Romeo, Robert Browning and Morrell, respectively.

The try-out for Broadway was held in Miss Cornell's home city of Buffalo, New York State, and would be the start of an arduous seven-month tour of eighty-six US cities during which the sold-out signs were posted at virtually every venue. Basil had to fight off a nasty bout of tonsillitis in the opening week, all but losing his voice but still managing to perform to his usual peerless standards. The show won immediate praise and would prove to be a huge success, enhancing Basil's reputation yet further as a classical actor.

Ouida was his constant companion, with the throat issue plaguing him throughout the tour eased only by medication and continuous spoonfuls of honey administered by his wife. In June 1934, he had the troublesome tonsils removed permanently. Refreshed by a much-needed spell on the stage, he once again felt ready to return to the movies. His return to the silver screen began with a part he felt was too good to turn down.

Though his agent informed him he had been offered the role of Pontius Pilate in *The Last Days of Pompeii*, the one-week schedule initially led him to turn the role down.

However, upon reading the script, he told his agent to get him the part no matter what. Filming began and Basil duly gave a masterly performance as Pilate.

In a *Motion Picture* magazine interview, he recalled fondly:

Yes, I think it's the best thing I have done on the screen, and perhaps the best thing I've done in my life. When I returned to Hollywood my manager said, 'Basil, they want you to play Pontius Pilate in *The Last Days of Pompeii*. It's a week's work.' I told him I wouldn't even consider a week's work. He wanted me to read the script, as a favour to him. I got the script with the part of Pontius Pilate all marked out. As I read it, I had cold shivers running up and down my spine. I called my manager and said, 'Bill, I was wrong. Get that part for me whatever you do.' It was magnificently written, with economy of words – truly a sublime characterization. I played the part, and the director will tell you that everything you saw on the screen was the first take. Not because I was a good boy and learned my lines, or a superlative actor, but because the part was me, and I was the part.

The *New York Times* review claimed: 'The hero of the occasion is Basil Rathbone, whose Pilate is a fascinating aristocrat, scornful in his hauteur and sly in his reasoning.'

The movie, directed by Ernest B. Schoedsack and Merian C. Cooper of *King Kong* fame, was a triumph, using the vast RKO Radio studio sets to spectacular effect in this most lavish production. It again proved Basil's versatility and though it initially lost $237,000, it was something of a slow burner, earning a re-release several years later and eventually turning a profit.

Next up was the melodrama *A Feather in Her Hat*, also released in 1935 by Colombia Pictures. But although it was backed by American dollars, it was filmed in London and didn't travel particularly well across the Atlantic, where critics were generally receptive of what was a gentle tale of a self-sacrificing mother seeking a better life for her son.

Despite the moderate showing of *A Feather in Her Hat*, 1935 would prove something of a golden year for Rathbone with his performance as the tyrannical Marquis de St Evremonde in Charles Dickens's *A Tale of Two Cities* earning him yet more widespread acclaim, not to mention a nomination for the American Film Institute's '100 Heroes and Villains' list. The film was a worldwide success, making more than $1,068,000 in box office profits.

As ever, the increasingly typecast Rathbone was exceptional in his latest villainous role, delivering lines such as the contemptuous outburst to a group of villagers after running over and killing a child. The spiteful Marquis addresses the gathering peasants, whom he regularly describes as pigs and vermin, by saying: 'It is extraordinary to me, that you people cannot take care of yourselves and your children. One or the other of you is forever in the way. How do I know what injury you have done my horses?'

It seemed whichever part he played, it had been especially written for him – of course, this was down to his skill as an actor – and while he was just as adept at playing the handsome lead in a romantic movie, he seemed to relish the less popular roles that he embraced wholeheartedly and with such regularity.

However, his next picture would not merely enhance his ability to portray the foulest of characters, it almost ended his career for good. With Charles Dickens quite the flavour of the year in Hollywood, *A Tale of Two Cities* producer David O. Selznick was keen to again surround himself with the best talent available, and that included Basil Rathbone, who was offered the role of the loathsome Edward Murdstone in *David Copperfield*.

With a stellar cast headed by the legendary W.C. Fields, Lionel Barrymore and Maureen O'Sullivan, the film proved a triumph. Basil had been reluctant to take on another brutal role so soon after the Marquis. In an interview in *Motion Picture*, he revealed his resistance was gradually worn down by a refusal to accept his decision by Selznick and director George Cukor. Though he felt he didn't have the stomach to play Murdstone, he eventually accepted the role and, as always, excelled.

'You can't play a man who's poison to you,' he said:

I refused the part of Murdstone five times and finally took it as one takes any desperate chance – with my heart quaking and my fingers crossed. I was to play the cold, cruel Mr Murdstone, and one morning at MGM I thrashed the living daylights out of poor little Freddie Bartholomew who was playing David Copperfield. It was a most unpleasant experience, for I was directed by Mr George Cukor to express no emotion whatsoever – merely to thrash the child to within an inch of his life! I had a vicious cane with much whip to it, but fortunately for Freddie Bartholomew and myself, under his britches and completely covering his little rump, he was protected by a sheet of foam rubber. Nevertheless, Freddie howled with pain (mostly anticipatory I presume) and in his close-ups his face was distorted, and he cried real tears most pitifully. As Mr Murdstone I tried to make my mind a blank, thrashing Freddie as hard as I could but like a machine. From time to time George Cukor would call for another 'take.' 'Basil,' he would say, 'you were thinking of something. Please don't – all right, let's try again!' Freddie and I became great friends, and he was often over to our house for a swim in the pool and dinner. This made the playing of Mr Murdstone all the harder for me.

The end product was a movie that Basil found difficult to watch, perhaps concerned by his own convincing performance of such a cruel character.

He added:

> I even hated George Cukor at times – childishly, illogically – for
> the things he made me do. Whatever credit's due belongs not to
> me, but to him. He can get anything out of anyone – the tender-
> est sentiment, the bitterest cruelty. He wanted cruelty from me,
> and he got it.
>
> When the picture was released, I received good reviews and a
> very heavy fan mail – all of it abusive! Mr Cukor and I had done
> our job well, so well that for some considerable time I was to
> become a victim of one of motion pictures' worst curses, 'typing.'
> I was now typed as 'a heavy' or villain, a category that often did
> not do justice to the role it was supposed, so arbitrarily, to define.

Variety, the *New Yorker* and the *New York Times* all praised the picture as
one of the best of the year and it went on to make over $3 million at
the box office – more than three times the $1 million it cost to make.

And hate mail or not, it further enhanced Basil's reputation as the
man everyone loved to hate. He was steadily boxing himself into a
corner and at that point, it was interesting to see what his next move
would be.

11

1935–1937

Swashbuckling Away in Hollywood

I am a man of fortune, and must seek my fortune …

Captain Henry Avery

Though Basil was again offered the role of the rather dour, convention-bound role of Karenin in the epic Tolstoy tale of *Anna Karenina*, it would prove to be one of the most enjoyable films of his career. Playing the husband of the protagonist, Anna, he also got to appear alongside movie legend Greta Garbo, which he found a most enlightening – and on at least one occasion deflating – experience.

He would learn much from Garbo during shooting, but he wasn't in full agreement that his latest movie cast him – yet again – as 'the heavy'. Indeed, he fully immersed himself in the part, believing the character's actions to be understandable and completely reasonable.

He wrote in his autobiography:

Here, in the making of this picture, is the almost perfect example of a loss of integrity that becomes inevitable when a single label is tabbed to a character of many dimensions. Karenin is not a heavy, a motion picture term that Tolstoy would have shuddered to hear defined. Anna had married Karenin of her own free will: they have a son, a boy of about ten years old. She falls in love with a very attractive young man, Vronsky, who is more of her age, Karenin being somewhat older than Anna. That she had fallen out of love with Karenin might be held much to Karenin's account. But he had not been cruel or unkind, rather he had been insensitive and possessive, and without much imagination. His faults are quite evident, and Tolstoy does not spare him. That Anna should have fallen in love with Vronsky was quite understandable to all except of course Karenin. But surely this does not make him a villain.

He added, during an interview with *Motion Picture*:

Karenin is a human being – a man whose point of view you can see even though you don't wholly sympathize with it. To me he's an even more tragic figure than Anna – for there's no greater tragedy than that of the person who feels but is so bound by convention that he can't give expression to his feeling. I can understand him. I can put myself into his shoes as I couldn't into Murdstone's, and I've never been so happy or at ease in any picture.

I had what many would call a brutal and merciless part as the husband, yet it is a character that is real. No caricature there! My own attitude toward Karenin is that he was a man who honoured the institution of marriage, and there was no brutality about him. He was an upstanding citizen, married to a very physical wife, whose tragedy was nothing compared to his. He is, indeed, the central character of the story. I should like to play it again!

Despite his own numerous successes, Basil was fascinated by the uber-cool Garbo and claimed to study the Swedish-born superstar during production. Though he had previously met her and spent time chatting, eating and even swimming with her at a mutual friend's home five or six years earlier, Garbo never once mentioned the previous meeting or acknowledged as much. Indeed, when he plucked up the courage to ask her to sign a photograph in between takes – a tradition he had with actors and actresses he admired – she said simply, 'I don't sign pictures!'

Aside from this, he would learn much from her acting methods and he would use the study of her ways for the rest of his career. He said:

> Before I played Karenin, I was puzzled about the technique of film acting, and wasn't satisfied at all with what I had been doing. During the filming of *Anna Karenina*, I watched Garbo and learned from her what I think is the secret of good screen acting; play your part with the least possible physical movement and the greatest possible mental projection. It is different on the stage. There your whole body is constantly exposed to the audience and you must have perfect coordination from head to foot. Physical movement is far more important on the stage than it is in films. In films mental projection means everything. And Garbo has this power of mental projection to a superb degree. I learned from her how little to do in order to get the greatest results. My work improved one hundred per-cent [*sic*]. Now, when I play a part, subconsciously I ask myself: What would Garbo do with this?

It was quite a statement that his work improved beyond recognition – in his opinion – given his already impressive body of work.

Graham Greene, reviewing the film in *The Spectator* magazine, was impressed by Garbo's powerful performance, writing: 'It is Greta Garbo's personality which "makes" this film, which fills the mould of the neat respectful adaptation with some kind of sense of the greatness of the novel.'

He went on to opine that Garbo's performance overwhelmed the rest of the cast… save for that of Basil Rathbone.

Anna Karenina earned Garbo the New York Critics Circle Award for Best Actress, as well as winning the Mussolini Cup for best foreign film at the Venice Film Festival. It also took a healthy $2.3 million at the box office. In short, it was another wise career move for Basil who had more than held his own alongside Hollywood royalty. The question was – what next? The offers were flooding in and Basil could afford to pick and choose his parts.

So, what better way to cast away the shackles of typecasting than with a good old blood-and-thunder pirate movie? Warner Brothers' *Captain Blood* would prove to be every bit the swashbuckling epic the moviegoing public were thirsty for, with a cast of soon to become Hollywood superstars such as Errol Flynn and Olivia de Havilland.

It wasn't a lead role for Basil, but it was a prominent one none-theless and allowed him to display his expertise as a swordsman in an epic fight scene with Flynn. During his time in the military, Rathbone had twice been crowned the British Army fencing champion, and he had honed his skills under the expert tutelage of former Olympic gold medallist Aldo Nadi and Hollywood fencing expert Fred Cavens – the latter believed Basil could have had a fine career as a competitive fencer.

Rathbone was the movie's biggest star, with Flynn and de Havilland virtual unknowns before the film was released. But the relatively rookie cast didn't stop the $1 million movie being a box office smash, raking in more than $2.5 million worldwide and making overnight stars of Flynn and de Havilland, while displaying Basil's diversity and athleticism in a role he clearly relished.

In an interview in *Castle of Frankenstein* magazine, Basil revealed:

> I enjoyed swordsmanship more than anything because it was beauti-ful. I thought it was a wonderful exercise, a great sport. But I would not put it under the category of sport; I would put it under the category of the arts. I think it's tremendously skilful and very beauti-ful. The only actor I actually fought with on the screen was Flynn, and that's the only time I was really scared. I wasn't scared because he was careless, but because he didn't know how to protect himself.

Inevitably cast as the (you guessed it) treacherous Captain Levasseur, at least this role was more colourful than some of his more recent heavies. Pirates were often portrayed as loveable rogues and as Captain Blood's partner, the role of Levasseur allowed Basil the opportunity to have some fun. The famous Flynn versus Rathbone sword fight was filmed at Laguna Beach in California and was one of the film's most memorable scenes. Basil had been given scant opportunity to show his diversity on the silver screen, so this was another feather in his cap and alerted Hollywood to his potential for more action movies.

Variety reviewed the movie, saying: '*Blood* is a spectacular cinematic entry, which, while not flawless, is quite compelling. Its sundry little discrepancies, however, count against a more satisfying final tally.'

Nominated for four Oscars, *Captain Blood* is still regarded as one of the best pirate movies ever made, and even today the sword fight is considered one of the most thrilling in cinema history.

Basil's next projects were *Kind Lady*, which added to his list of 1935 MGM movies, and *Private Number* early in 1936, both of which were steady and unspectacular. He then began filming one of the stories he loved the most, *Romeo and Juliet*. Sadly, at the age of 43, the opportunity came a decade too late and Basil's days of playing one of his most beloved roles in Romeo were over, and he instead took a supporting part. Had the movie version of Shakespeare's play happened sooner in his career, it would undoubtedly have propelled Basil into becoming a major Hollywood star far quicker, for he is still widely considered to have given some of the best portrayals of a role he had perfected over close to two decades.

Produced by the legendary Irving Thalberg, who cast his wife Norma Shearer as Juliet, the lavish production would earn more than $2 million and still make a sizeable loss, and though reviews were mixed, it resulted in Basil's first Oscar nomination as Best Supporting Actor for his portrayal of Tybalt. Thalberg was nominated for Best Picture and his wife Norma for Best Actress, but tragedy was about to strike the Rathbones' close friend Thalberg, producer of epics such as *Mutiny on the Bounty* and *Ben-Hur* when, on the night of the film's Los Angeles premiere, he died, aged only 37, of pneumonia.

Basil later wrote:

Irving Thalberg was one of the most sensitive men I have ever met. Slight of build, good-looking, and very intelligent, he drove himself unmercifully. It is said that he had a premonition of his early and most regrettable death, and his determination to accomplish the impossible obsessed every minute of his life. Most certainly his production of *Romeo and Juliet* in 1935 had a physical beauty, an integrity and inspiration that places it among the all-time greats. And I doubt that any picture has had or will ever have such a distinguished and memorable cast.

A month or so after the tragic passing of Irving, *Romeo and Juliet* was released in London and I happened to be there and was asked to speak at its opening. A London newspaper of October 15, 1936, reported, 'Incidentally I thought Basil Rathbone struck entirely the right note in making his speech from the stage a tribute to Irving Thalberg. The great producer has been associated with many great films, but this was entirely his. It was his last film; the star was his wife; and the subject is entirely true to that betterment of the screen which was his unceasing aim.'

The 1930s had so far been kind to the prolific Basil Rathbone who, before the new decade began, would make another thirteen pictures at an average of almost one every three months. Some would be memorable, some not so much, and one would be a box office smash that would reunite Basil with his swashbuckling pals from *Captain Blood*, Errol Flynn and Olivia de Havilland, by now major Hollywood stars in their own right … exciting times lay ahead.

12

1937–1938

Horror at Los Feliz Boulevard

'If there are no dogs in Heaven, then when I die, I want to go where they went.'

Will Rogers

After completing another well-received David Selznick movie, *The Garden of Allah*, in which Basil starred alongside Charles Boyer and Marlene Dietrich, the Rathbones sailed to England where filming for the United Artists picture *Love from a Stranger* would begin. Before they set sail from New York to Southampton, Ouida threw a lavish cocktail party at the Lombardy Hotel where they had based themselves for several weeks. They would remain in England for a couple of months during filming, before spending time in Paris and Budapest on a brief European sojourn and returning to New York on Christmas Eve, where they would spend the festive period at The Lombardy. Then, it was back to Hollywood and the charming property on Los Feliz Boulevard near Glendale that Basil and Ouida had initially rented for three months, but had by then been their Los Angeles residence for almost three years. It was a happy place and time for the Rathbones, and between filming Basil would play tennis, golf with David Niven, listen to music, walk and play with their three dogs or just enjoy the company of his wife. Basil claimed he was of little interest to the paparazzi because he led such a boring life! It was hardly that, but he and Ouida rarely ventured out to late-night parties and Basil most certainly preferred a quiet life, taking long walks and relaxing whenever he could.

Their close friend Jack Miltern had become a regular companion and a good sounding board for both. Now in his mid-60s, he had come to live with them and stayed in the studio apartment above the garage. After a decade of hard work, Basil and Ouida were taking a much-needed break. Basil wrote:

> Above and beyond everything, Ouida and I were free to enjoy a long overdue postgraduate honeymoon. Many were the sacrifices Ouida had made for me in this journeying we had planned together and in the directing of my professional life, and we fell in love again, as it were, in this Garden of another was deserving of this time we had earned together, and we were in need of the time to enjoy one another again, released as we were, at last, from the pressures and burdens that are inherent in the building of any successful career.

Make no mistake, Basil felt he owed Ouida everything and was convinced his career would have floundered without her. Of all their time together, it was during this period that they were at their happiest. Life was good for the Rathbones, but as had been the case on numerous occasions in Basil's life, tragedy was just around the corner, and on this occasion it would be in the form of the horrific death of Jack Miltern and a bizarre episode almost immediately after the accident which, if Basil recalled the whole episode correctly, was inexplicable.

He recalled the horror in his autobiography:

> We had started out on this day for our usual walk with the dogs, a little later than usual. The sun was setting. It was a beautiful evening. Ouida had come running to the garden gate to call us back

to go with her in the car for a drive to watch the sun set into the Pacific. But we had gone just too far to hear her calling – or had we? How much of destiny is there in events such as these? This was the day and the hour and destiny was not to be denied by anything as fragile as the human will to live. The sky was bright and clear – an eternity above us. The dogs were soon hunting, and Jack and I followed the paths we had trod so often together while Ouida jumped into her car and drove off to the ocean. Jack had Leo, Bunty and Cullum. I had Moritza and Happy and Judy. The traffic was heavy on Los Feliz Boulevard as we waited to cross the road to our house. Suddenly, with no obvious reason, Jack walked out into the road. I screamed at him to wait and a moment later he and his three dogs were hit by a passing car. I saw them, all four of them, in the air, and a few seconds later, four motionless bodies lay in the road, some ten to fifteen yards distant. The cars didn't stop, they just slowed down and went around, the motionless bodies. I was powerless to move. I yelled at the passing traffic for help and at last a car stopped beside Jack, who was bleeding profusely.

Though Jack was still alive on the way to hospital, he died soon after, leaving Basil to tell Ouida on her return from watching the sunset. At first, she was quiet and clearly couldn't take it in, instead commenting on the beautiful sunset she had witnessed. The tears would come later. While the couple were still coming to terms with their loss, the phone rang, and Basil answered it.

He recalled:

A woman's voice spoke. 'Am I speaking to Mr Rathbone?' she asked. 'This is he,' I replied. 'You don't know me,' she continued. 'I am not a medium or anything like that, but I have what I think you might call extrasensory perception or something. These things happen to me once in a while. I don't know why. They just happen.'

'What is it?' I asked.

'Did you lose someone very dear to you a short while ago?'

'Yes. Why?' I inquired.

'Well, he has asked me to get in touch with you and tell you he's all right. He said he wouldn't be able to contact me again because he is moving on very fast, but please to tell you – and oh yes – he said to be sure and tell you there were no dogs where he is – does it make any sense?'

'It does indeed,' I replied, 'and I am deeply grateful to you. May I ask to whom I am talking?'

'I would rather not if you don't mind. I am not a professional or anything like that. These things just happen to me and I feel it my duty to do as I'm asked.'

'But how did you get my number?'

'I called all the studios and got it at last from Warner Brothers. I told them I had urgent news for you of a dear friend who had died. I couldn't very well say from someone who was dead! Anyway, it wouldn't have been true because you see he isn't dead, only to you, and only then for a while until you understand. You do understand, don't you?'

'Of course, I do.'

'And you do believe me, don't you?'

'Of course, I do – and God bless you. Good night.'

The phone call had a profound effect on Basil, who, with some justification, argued that nobody other than the emergency services would have been aware of Jack's death, with the window of time being too brief. He chose to believe the call had been genuine and took great comfort from it. The loss made the Rathbones decide to leave Los Feliz Boulevard and find a new home. One of Jack's dogs, Leo, who had survived the accident and had never left his side while his master was alive, never slept in his bedroom again. Through their front windows, there was a constant reminder of those terrible events and Basil could never cross the road outside again without thinking of that horrific day. Only a move away would ease the pain.

Just a day after losing Jack, Basil was a pallbearer at another family friend's funeral, that of Richard Boleslawski, director of *The Garden of Allah*, who passed away aged only 47.

At least there was one bright light on the horizon around this time. After years of hoping, Basil would finally have the chance to get to know his son Rodion properly, after he told his father he was coming to Hollywood to live with him for a while. Now 22, Rodion had graduated from Cambridge University and was ready to try and get closer to his father of whom, in spite of their chequered past, he was immensely proud. Prior to his arrival, in a feature called 'Secret Families', published in the June 1937 edition of *Silver Screen*, Basil was interviewed about his son's imminent arrival. He said:

> The boy followed my father's footsteps rather than mine in his education, by becoming an electrical engineer, but the acting profession intrigues him tremendously and he may try his luck on the screen. I would be very proud were he to become an actor and shall encourage him, but the final decision will be his. One must choose his own career if he is to be happy in it. Whatever comes from this visit, I shall have the great joy of his companionship and, at last, my son will be a reality. This is something I've dreamed about for many years.

Life went on and Basil continued to make movies, with *Confession*, *Tovarich* and *Make A Wish* all released in 1937. None particularly advanced his career, but they paid well, and by the same token didn't do his reputation any harm with his portrayal generally praised in each picture, particularly *Make A Wish* in which he was given the rare opportunity to play the lead in a relaxed, light-hearted movie. His first picture of 1938, *The Adventures of Marco Polo*, was Samuel Goldwyn's epic and expensive tale in which Basil portrayed the conniving Ahmed, but the choice of Hollywood leading man Gary Cooper, a huge film star at the time but undoubtedly miscast on this occasion, largely proved to be the film's downfall, with the picture receiving mixed reviews and making a substantial loss.

At home, Rodion had spent more time with his father than ever before and the pair had managed to form a blossoming relationship.

He had also met a young, upcoming actress named Caroline Fisher while living in Bel Air and after a whirlwind romance, the couple announced they were to be married. Ouida, the Hollywood hostess par excellence, duly took the reins. She decided she would give the young couple a wedding they would never forget, and it would be held at the Rathbones' family home with a guest list that read like a Hollywood premiere. But Ouida's overpowering personality and determination to do things her way would go disastrously wrong and leave Basil's relationship with Rodion in shreds in the process.

Ouida Rathbone staged a grand Hollywood wedding reception for Rodion and Caroline in the garden of the Rathbone home in the spring of 1938. A-lister Hollywood stars came to the party and the movie fan magazines published photos of the celebrities at Ouida's event. However, Rodion and Caroline felt that they should have been the centre of attention at their own wedding, and not just part of the background. This led to simmering resentment.

According to Rodion's son, his parents didn't feel that their wedding day was their special day. The reception was all about the Hollywood movie stars in attendance. The photographers were busy taking pictures of the celebrities. Gary Cooper even chided one photographer, 'Why are you photographing me? I'm not the groom!'

The young couple felt somewhat slighted, the supporting act at their own wedding, as Ouida did her thing in a way only Ouida could. In Ouida's mind, this party was her great gift to them, and Rodion and Caroline owed a debt of gratitude to her.

Years later, Dounia Rathbone, Rodion's daughter, revealed: 'Ouida gave the newlywed couple a house in Hollywood, completely furnished, as a wedding present. My mother, being who she was, declined this "generous" gift – golden handcuffs come to mind.'

This was the final straw for Ouida. Not only, in her eyes, had they not shown adequate appreciation of her efforts, they were turning down her once-in-a-lifetime wedding present. It was a tinderbox situation, and given how strongly Rodion and Caroline felt about the whole affair, a furious argument ensued. This difference of opinion led, inevitably, to an explosive conclusion with Rodion and

Caroline on one side, and Ouida and Basil on the other. After the heated exchange, Basil told Rodion that he never wanted to see him again. It's doubtful he meant it so literally, but the words couldn't be taken back.

As a result, Rodion and Caroline left the Rathbone household, and soon moved more than 2,000 miles east to Chicago. Except for one occasion two decades in the future, Rodion did not see his father again. Sadly, as a result, his children did not have a relationship with their grandfather. It was a wound that would never fully heal for either man. Basil had left Rodion as a young boy and now Rodion had been ordered to leave by his father. He had chosen to side with Ouida instead of his own flesh and blood, and all the time and effort both had made trying to have a loving father-and-son relationship was wasted.

As ever, Basil threw himself into his work to deal with the upset, and his next picture would undoubtedly be one of his best as he struck gold in Sherwood Forest …

From the film *A Woman Commands*.

Basil Rathbone, Boris Karloff and Donnie Dunagan in the film *Son of Frankenstein*.

Basil Rathbone and Donnie Dunagan, from the film *Son of Frankenstein*.

Boris Karloff and Basil Rathbone, celebrating Boris's birthday on the set of the film *Son of Frankenstein*.

Basil Rathbone and Olivia de Havilland, from the film *The Adventures of Robin Hood*.

Basil Rathbone and his son Rodion Rathbone on the set of *The Dawn Patrol*.

Photo produced for the 1953 play *Sherlock Holmes*. Text on back reads: 'Bust by Albert Silva of the Special Effects Dept. of Paramount Studios'.

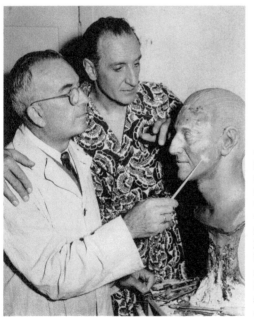

Another photo produced for the 1953 play *Sherlock Holmes*. Text on the back reads: 'Basil Rathbone poses for an exact life-size model of himself which will be used this fall on Broadway when he portrays "Sherlock Holmes" for the first time on the stage in the Bill Doll production of the new play based on the adventures of the world's most famous detective. Paramount Studios sculptor Albert Silva puts some finishing touches to his facsimile of the actor.'

Basil Rathbone in the role of Mr Zuss in the play *J.B.* (Photo by Friedman-Abeles)

Basil Rathbone and Helen Menken in the play *The Captive*. (Photo by Florence Vandamm)

Basil Rathbone and Mary Nash in the play *The Command to Love*. (Photo by White Studio)

Basil Rathbone and Dorothy Cumming in the play *Judas*.

Basil Rathbone, Mae Murray and Francis X. Bushman in the film *The Masked Bride*.

Ann Harding and Basil Rathbone taking tea together on their first day at the studio where they made *Love from a Stranger*. (Photo by Trafalgar Films)

Basil Rathbone and
Ann Harding, from the
film *Love from a Stranger*

Basil Rathbone and Ruth Chatterton, from the film *The Lady of Scandal*.

Basil Rathbone and an unidentified actor, from the film *A Tale of Two Cities*.

Basil Rathbone and Nigel Bruce, from the film *The Adventures of Sherlock Holmes*.

Basil Rathbone and Ida Lupino, from the film *The Adventures of Sherlock Holmes*.

Basil Rathbone with fencing master and trainer Fred Cavens.

Basil Rathbone, Ouida and their dog Moritz. The photo is undated, but estimated at around 1927.

Basil Rathbone and Aileen Pringle, from the film *The Great Deception*.

Basil Rathbone with Norma Shearer and George Barraud, from the film *The Last of Mrs Cheyney*.

Basil Rathbone in the film *The Bishop Murder Case*.

Basil Rathbone and his daughter Cynthia. The photo is undated, but the photographer was based in New York, so it was taken after 1946. (Photo by Edward Ozern)

Basil Rathbone and his daughter Cynthia in 1954. Text on back reads: 'Basil Rathbone escorts Cynthia, his daughter, to a film first night in Hollywood. Photo by Nat Dallinger. Copyright 1954, King Features Syndicate, Inc.'

Ladies meeting at the Rathbone home to plan a charity ball, April 1939.
Seating order is unclear, but the ladies are: Joan Bennett, Janet Gaynor, Ouida
Rathbone, Mrs E.G. Robinson, Mrs Jesse Lasky, Mrs Jules Stein.

Basil Rathbone as
Sherlock Holmes.

Basil Rathbone and Nigel Bruce as Sherlock Holmes and Dr Watson.

A postcard signed by Basil Rathbone and dated 'Dec. 25, 1913'.

Basil Rathbone and Errol Flynn, from the film *The Dawn Patrol*.

Basil Rathbone and Beatrice Straight in the play *The Heiress*. This photo is from the USA tour. Beatrice Straight did not play the role of the daughter on Broadway. (Photo by Vandamm)

13

1938–1939

Hollywood's Evermore Reluctant Villain

What's important about an actor is his acting, not his life.

Vincent Price

Nobody played the bad guy like Basil Rathbone, and the opportunities to take on different personas on screen were few and far between. He was just too good at portraying cold-hearted, cruel and venomous characters. Though handsome and debonair, he was never going to compete for the roles Errol Flynn and Charles Boyer would land, though he was perfect as their nemesis.

He was rarely approached to play the loving family man or the hero. At least, not yet. It was just how he was perceived. During a movie called *The Ghost Chasers* with Bob Hope, in the background thunder and lightning strikes a nearby building, and Hope says, 'Ah, Basil Rathbone must be throwing a party.'

Somehow, with each villainous role, he managed to give the character another dimension and could never have been accused of playing the same character over and over. At least not yet.

The 1938 production of *The Adventures of Robin Hood* was one of Basil's greatest pictures and proved a worldwide box office smash.

In many ways, the part of Sir Guy of Gisbourne could only have been played by Basil Rathbone and for all the remakes of *Robin Hood* over the years, no actor has come even close to portraying the hero's archenemy with such venomous delight.

The decision to reunite Errol Flynn, Olivia de Havilland and Rathbone was inspired and Warner Brothers splashed out $2 million to create a movie that laid the foundations for future adventure epics such as *Indiana Jones* in years to come.

With Bidwell Park in California standing in for Sherwood Forest, filming began on *Robin Hood*, Warner Brothers' most ambitious project yet, but the investment paid off handsomely with worldwide box office takings of $4 million, making it the sixth biggest grossing movie of the year.

Basil is very much in his element throughout and the sword fight with Flynn was a triumph and proved to be the movie's most memorable scene. The reviews were excellent, and though Flynn won the majority of praise, Rathbone deservedly won many plaudits in what many claimed was the film of the year, and which would go on to win three Oscars.

Lapped up by the critics and moviegoers alike, this tour-de-force action yarn placed Basil as the undisputed king of Hollywood bad guys – in short, the man everyone loved to hate was simply too good at playing the man who appeared to hate everyone.

For such a popular, gregarious actor, it was a curious juxtaposition to be in, especially as he was approaching the height of his fame. Did he begin turning down these meaty, memorable parts and wait for something that was more palatable? Or did he make hay while the sun shone?

Of course, he could always return to his first love, theatre, but it paid a third or less of the salary he would earn for one picture, and there was always the chance the production would close early. Plus, as the sole breadwinner, there was an element of pressure to keep Ouida in the life she and he were accustomed to – particularly as she continued to throw expensive parties on a fairly regular basis.

From May through to June, Basil filmed *If I Were King*, playing King Louis XI, giving a superb performance which was reviewed in the *Hollywood* magazine by Llewellyn Miller, who wrote:

On the screen Rathbone has created a living character, complete with one of the best cackles it has been our privilege to hear, a nervous grimace, a different way of walking, a voice unlike any he has used before. He has created a subtle, disillusioned, shrewd and shrewish old nobleman who bewilders a beggar by giving him kingly power… and a death sentence.

Released in November 1938, it led to Basil's second Oscar nomination, this time for Best Actor in a Supporting Role, though the prize would go to Walter Brennan for his role in *Kentucky*.

And the memorable roles kept coming, with the First World War movie *The Dawn Patrol* seeing Basil again appearing alongside Errol Flynn and his good friend David Niven. Filmed before the family split and released on Christmas Eve 1938, it would also be the first film that Basil's son Rodion appeared in with his father, but it would have an odd effect on Basil.

Hollywood magazine reported: 'He claims appearing with Rodion was the most unusual, unnerving experience in his life and when he had to play a scene in *Dawn Patrol* opposite his son who had been cast as a recruit, Basil became so confused that he blew up in his lines.'

The scene in the movie, in which Rodion was effectively sent on a mission he would never return from, was changed at Basil's request. Even in a film, he couldn't send his son to certain doom. Rodion was credited as 'John Rodion', but the scene was cut. It was one of just two films Rodion appeared in as he attempted to follow his father into acting.

The Dawn Patrol saw Basil at his very best, playing the role of a commanding officer of a squadron of the British Royal Flying Corps, and he clearly drew heavily on his own wartime experiences to give a stunning performance that many believed should have earned him an Oscar. Despite the stellar cast, it was Rathbone who was lauded in the reviews that followed its release.

Variety wrote: 'Basil Rathbone is superb as the aviator who suffers inwardly the loss of every man while he is forced to remain in command on the ground.'

Modern Screen added: 'Basil Rathbone, as the British squadron commander whose job it is to send these boys into the slaughter, gives a memorable performance.'

Other reviews claimed that Basil Rathbone had further cemented his place among Hollywood's leading men and that, for once, his performance overshadowed Errol Flynn – perhaps because, for the first time, they were actually on the same side!

The Dawn Patrol was well received by critics and moviegoers and it made a healthy profit at the festive box office, being one of the holiday season's biggest hits. Costing $500,000 to make, it made just shy of $2.2 million worldwide and capped the best year of Basil Rathbone's career, during which he had given three performances which were each deemed by critics as worthy of an Oscar. Quite an accolade.

Some years later, Basil would say of Flynn:

God gave him the most beautiful body. He's intelligent. He can act. He arrived very fast. He arrived almost overnight. And he simply wasn't ready, he wasn't sufficiently well disciplined in life to know that he had to conform. Now he has made non-conformity a sort-of idiosyncrasy. It's now almost a big bluff, because he's thrown a very wonderful career out of the window.

As if to illustrate the point, in the book *Basil Rathbone: His Life and His Films*, the author Michael Druxman writes:

The Rathbones gained a reputation for throwing lavish (and expensive!) parties, which the biggest stars in Hollywood attended. At one such party Errol Flynn got drunk, followed a young lady home and passed out on her living room sofa. Later that night, the woman's father brought the unconscious Flynn back to the Rathbones' house and dumped him on the lawn. The next morning, Basil and Ouida were having breakfast on the patio, when the gardener turned on the sprinklers. Who should spring up from the grass, but a hung-over Errol Flynn? The Rathbones sat – mouths agape – as Errol bid them a cheery 'Good morning,' then departed for home.

Flynn undoubtedly did things his way, but he was indeed seemingly hellbent on self-destruction.

Meanwhile, Basil was at the peak of his powers and it seemed nothing could stop his steady ascent to worldwide fame. He had also, at least for the time being, managed to shake the shackles of being typecast and must have felt liberated by the variety of roles he had been offered.

Proof, if needed, was evident in perhaps a new-found freedom as he next appeared alongside horror legends Boris Karloff and Bela Lugosi in Universal's *Son of Frankenstein*, the rip-roaring third movie of the *Frankenstein* franchise. Universal had ceased making horror flicks for a few years, feeling the genre was tired, and so the careers of Karloff and Lugosi temporarily went into freefall.

But a decision by a Californian theatre to put a horror double-bill of Lugosi's *Dracula* and Karloff's *Frankenstein* caught the studio by complete surprise. Moviegoers queued around the block to watch the films, and the double feature was given a wider release and was the surprise box office smash of the year. The result was that horror was very much back on the menu and *Son of Frankenstein* proved the perfect main course for bloodthirsty horror fans. Had Peter Lorre not been suffering from ill-health at the time of shooting, Basil would never have got the part – he was, in fact, the studio's second choice – but it proved an inspired one.

Donnie Dunagan, a child actor who would famously go on to be the voice of Disney's Bambi, played Basil's son Peter, and he recalled how Universal bosses attempted to cash in on Lugosi's precarious financial state at the time by offering him a fraction of the fees Karloff and Rathbone were receiving. When Basil and Karloff discovered this, they demanded Lugosi be paid a fee that matched his standing – and, eventually, the studio conceded and paid him the fee he deserved. Lugosi responded with arguably his greatest performance yet.

Recalled Dunagan:

I felt very fortunate to be working with Mr Rathbone and Mr Karloff. Rathbone was an absolute capital fellow. He would sometimes read to me during long breaks, usually from Kipling.

Now, he didn't have to do that – that just shows what a good guy he was. And Karloff was a very sweet and sensitive man. I could sense that he was an accomplished stage actor, but he was this rugged-looking guy who got typecast in these horror roles.

Basil plays Baron Wolf von Frankenstein, with Karloff playing The Monster and Lugosi stealing the show as Ygor. The 1939 release was a box office smash and yet another feather in the cap of Rathbone as he appeared, and more than held his own, alongside two of the genre's genuine legends.

Son of Frankenstein, many believe, was the best of the 1930s *Frankenstein* trilogy of movies. And it would also prove to be the final time Karloff played 'The Monster', as he feared more portrayals would see the character become the butt of jokes and, in many ways, he would be proved correct.

Rathbone then appeared as Edward III in *Tower of London*, appearing again with Karloff and Vincent Price in another triumphant role. Such was his demand that he filmed *Rio* at the same time. It was high times indeed.

Vincent Price enjoyed working with Basil immensely. In an interview later that year, he said:

> Basil was one of the nicest men that ever lived. I did a picture with him called *Tower of London* and years ago, he was Richard III and was absolutely marvellous in it. And he did a wonderful thing, sort of to keep everybody's spirits up. He got us all together, all the cast – being the star, he could do this – and he said, 'Let's make an agreement amongst ourselves. Let's never tell a dirty joke that we didn't hear after we were fourteen.' Well, we'd all go home at night and think of all the dirty jokes that we'd heard before we were fourteen. They weren't particularly dirty, but they were really funny. We'd come on set the next day and tell all these stories. Basil was a sweet man – a great prankster and joker, but a wonderful actor.

It was just before the end of the decade when Basil visited Sir Frank Benson back in England, who, by that time, had dramatically fallen from grace. Now 81, Sir Frank was dying and the blood link between him and Basil turned out to be far more diluted than generally imagined. It turned out Basil was Sir Frank's third cousin, once removed on his father's side – incredible considering how uncannily similar they looked when each had turned 30. It was to be a sad end for one of theatre's true pioneers.

Basil recalled:

At his death Sir Frank left me the sword he had been knighted with and all else of his worldly possessions. Sir Frank and Lady Benson both had money, as also did his brother Lord Charnwood, who invested liberally in Sir Frank's ventures. The last time I saw Sir Frank he was lying on an iron cot in a rooming house in the Holland Road, London. He was dying – alone – except for a few visitors like myself, and he was penniless, except for a government grant of a hundred pounds a year.

His marriage had broken up, and after his 'dismissal' from Stratford-on-Avon, he never had any further success. No businessman, he gradually fell into poverty, and then into virtual penury. He looked up at me from his deathbed for a long time without recognizing me. I tried to talk to him. At last he reached up and touched my face with an emaciated hand – he was eighty-one years old. There was the shadow of a smile in his eyes as he said just one word, 'Basil.'

Then once again he relapsed into semi-consciousness. A passionately dedicated young man – winner of the coveted three-mile race at Oxford University (a painting of him in his running shorts and his university colours still hangs to this day in the foyer of the Stratford Memorial Theatre). A 'successful' marriage – a fortune – nay, three – his own, his wife's, and his brother's – were poured into his beloved theatrical ventures. Could it have been that the death of his son, in France, during the war, had seriously affected his mind in some way? He seemed never quite to recover from this blow. He rarely spoke of it. And not until after his death did I know that I was to inherit all that was left of his worldly possessions – the sword with which he was knighted – a flowered costume vest – and a book of press clippings.

As one legendary member of the Rathbone clan passed away just hours before the new decade began, so another, the family's most famous son, powered forward with his career.

The Sun Never Sets, in which he starred alongside Douglas Fairbanks Junior, ended a prolific decade for Rathbone, but the threat of war meant the movie was somewhat overlooked by the American public. But, of course, it is necessary to backtrack slightly to the start of the year and a movie that would elevate Basil Rathbone's fame to new levels …

14

1939–1941

The Game's Afoot!

I never worked with a nicer man than Basil, and I never acted
with a more unselfish or more cooperative actor.

Nigel Bruce

There is a story that has been recounted many times in Hollywood.
It is, as they say, the stuff of legend, but undoubtedly true, and it
would change the lives of English actors Basil Rathbone and Nigel
Bruce forever.

One evening, when Twentieth Century Fox studio execu-
tive Darryl F. Zanuck – father of then 5-year-old Richard Zanuck,
who would later go on to produce the 1975 worldwide smash
Jaws – was entertaining friends (director Gregory Ratoff and writer
Gene Markey), the topic of Sherlock Holmes came up. Ratoff asked
Zanuck, 'Why don't you make a Holmes picture?'

Zanuck was immediately intrigued and said, 'Yes, but who can we
get to play Holmes?'

Markey looked surprised by the question. 'Who? Basil Rathbone,
of course!'

Zanuck then asked, 'But then we need Watson.'

Ratoff causally replied, 'My friend Nigel Bruce.'

'That sounds like something to go after – get them down here in the morning.'

No further discussion was needed.

Basil later recalled: 'Nigel Bruce and I were phoned by our agents to go over to Fox to discuss making *The Hound of the Baskervilles*. There was never any intention discussing anything other than "The Hound".'

But what chances that the perfect duo were also the best of friends in real life? Considering Basil was a natural choice, had nobody ever even considered he and Nigel Bruce would make the perfect crime-solving pair? It almost seems too coincidental, too perfect a fit.

Basil not only looked like the imagined character, he sounded as everyone imagined he would and had the intelligence and wit to carry off portraying the most famous (and loved) of fictional detectives.

In reality, there was no other actor who could play the role of Sherlock Holmes – Basil Rathbone had been born to play the part. What he couldn't have realised in accepting the part of Britain's most ingenious detective is the effect it would have on his career.

Sherlock Holmes would make Basil Rathbone an even bigger star than he already was, but ultimately, he would also make him very unhappy – though it would take several years before he tired of wearing the deerstalker and smoking a pipe.

Twentieth Century Fox had acquired the rights to the story, and though the end result would suggest the movie had been shot entirely on location on Devon's mysterious Dartmoor, filming never left California, with the brooding moors and Baskerville Hall all created on one of Fox's enormous back lots.

As for Basil, he could have literally played the super sleuth in his sleep. The part allowed him to bring many of the characteristics that had made him Hollywood's favourite villain into a part that while distant, superior and even cold, was also the hero who solved the unsolvable. Had Sir Arthur Conan Doyle written Holmes with an actor in mind, then surely it would have been Basil Rathbone.

Holmes had been on the big screen before, but none would play it better than Rathbone, with his voice and delivery giving life to the man so many millions had imagined and read about over the years.

As far as Rathbone was concerned, this was a one-off role – one to be enjoyed and explored. There was no hint that playing Sherlock Holmes would extend beyond *The Hound of the Baskervilles*. And he was excited to play a part that was so quintessentially English and held in such high esteem in his homeland.

After landing the role, he said:

> I think that Holmes is one of the greatest characters in fiction. With all the thousands of detective and mystery stories that have been written since, the name of Sherlock Holmes still stands at the head of the roster of famous sleuths. It is synonymous with the very word 'detective'. To play such a character means as much to me as ten Hamlets.

This would be the only Holmes film where Basil wasn't billed as the lead actor – upcoming English actor (and Devonian) Richard Greene was afforded that honour and the movie was, in many ways, seen as a vehicle for Greene to become Fox's heartthrob lead male.

Filming began early in 1939, and after an eight-week shoot the movie was released on 31 March that year. Surprisingly, it received a lukewarm reception in Britain, but proved to be a sizeable hit in the USA.

Nigel Bruce, who would play Holmes's entertaining sidekick, had been in a dark place following the failure of a project he'd been involved in, and prior to the offer of playing Dr Watson he could see little light at the end of the tunnel. He later joked that he was considering putting his head in an oven before he received a call from his old friend Basil Rathbone to come and play the part of Dr Watson.

Bruce later wrote:

> *The Hound of the Baskervilles*, which is perhaps Conan Doyle's most exciting adventure of Sherlock Holmes, was selected as the first vehicle for Basil and me. Much of the picture was made in a huge stage on the 20th-Century back lot.
>
> The entire stage was surrounded by a circular screen of canvas on which was painted a very lifelike picture of Dartmoor. The centre of the stage was filled with large boulders made of plaster

of Paris. Here and there a bridge was seen, and several caves were visible. Running through the boggy marsh-like ground were several small streams.

For eight weeks we worked in this set, and the atmosphere was most unpleasant as the fog which was necessary to the story was made by artificial methods and freshly pumped into the stage after every shot. The effect reached, however, was eerie and foreboding and the picture turned out to be an excellent one.

Basil Rathbone looked exactly like every picture that one has ever seen of Sherlock Holmes; and the cast, which was a good one, included Wendy Barrie, Lionel Atwill, John Carradine and an attractive young newcomer from England by the name of Richard Greene. Our director was Sidney Lanfield. Lanfield had the reputation of being a tartar, but after a few outbursts during the first few days, Basil and I got on splendidly with him. Each morning we greeted him with great affection and both of us would plant a kiss on his furrowed brow. After each take, we would shake hands and solemnly congratulate one another on our 'excellent performance'. We took the whole film in a mood of light-hearted enjoyment which left Sidney, who was accustomed to arguments and scenes, in a state of complete bafflement, and he gave up losing his temper in sheer self-defence. The result of this was that we all worked happily together and enjoyed every moment on the picture.

I never worked with a nicer man than Basil, and I never acted with a more unselfish or more cooperative actor.

The Baskervilles took from December 29th, 1938, to the 8th of March 1939, and in the picture, I earned nearly $10,000. *The Hound of the Baskervilles* was released… and its reception both in America and in England, where we felt they would be more critical, was beyond our wildest hopes. Basil was hailed as a splendid Sherlock Holmes and the critics not only gave him high praise but remarked that his resemblance to the general idea of the great detective was amazing. As Doctor Watson, I seemed to amuse and satisfy the many devoted admirers of the Conan Doyle characters.

The *London Sunday Pictorial* said this of the film: 'In my excitement I dropped my hat, cigarettes, gloves and matches, and I let them stay on the floor until the lights went up.'

Rathbone had enjoyed the experience of playing Holmes, adding:

Had I made but the one Holmes picture, my first, *The Hound of the Baskervilles*, I should probably not be as well-known as I am today. But within myself, as an artist, I should have been well content. Of all the 'adventures' *The Hound* is my favourite story, and it was in this picture that I had the stimulating experience of creating, within my own limited framework, a character that has intrigued me as much as any I have ever played.

The film was a huge success, both in America and internationally.

Hal Erickson of *Rovi* wrote: 'One of the best screen versions of this oft-told tale ... A big hit in a year of big hits, *The Hound of the Baskervilles* firmly established Basil Rathbone and Nigel Bruce as moviedom's definitive Sherlock Holmes and Dr Watson.'

Variety wrote:

Rathbone gives a most effective characterization of Sherlock Holmes which will be relished by mystery lovers. Greene, in addition to playing the intended victim of the murderer, is the romantic interest opposite Wendy Barrie.

Supporting cast is meritorious – mostly English players who fit neatly into individual roles. Group includes Nigel Bruce, Lionel Atwill, John Carradine, Barlowe Borland and Eily Malyon.

Chiller mood generated by the characters and story is heightened by effects secured from sequences in the medieval castle and the dreaded fog-bound moors. Low key photography by Peverell Marley adds to suspense in the unfolding.

Direction swings along at a deliberate and steady pace, catching every chance to add to the chiller-mystery tempo. Picture is rounded out nicely from the production end.

Silver Screen added: 'This mystery will have you holding on to your seats – It is indeed a pleasure to find Sherlock Holmes back on the screen this month. Especially when he is played by that grand actor Basil Rathbone, who is simply Mr Holmes to a T.'

Finally, *Motion Picture Daily* added:

> To the millions who know Sir Arthur Conan Doyle's *The Hound of the Baskervilles*, looking at the picture is like reading the book again. It follows the story almost page for page. To those unfamiliar with the story, the picture means attention-holding mystery melodrama.
>
> Not a horror picture in the accepted sense of the word, this adventure of Sherlock Holmes is appealing thrill entertainment into which has been woven ample romantic love interest and comedy. It does not feature any repulsive characters or situations that might make soft-hearted people wary of seeing it. Still, told against weird and eerie backgrounds, there is no lack of those elements that make the pulse beat a little faster and hold emotions in suspense.
>
> Featuring Basil Rathbone as Sherlock, Nigel Bruce as Dr Watson, Richard Greene, who shares the romantic love interest with Wendy Barrie and who participates in much of the melodrama; Lionel Atwill, John Carradine, Barlow Borland, Morton Lowry and Beryl Mercer, all of whom are convincing in their roles, the locale is a fog-hung moor in England's Devonshire country. For generations, heirs to the Baskerville estates have been terrorized to death. Holmes pitting his cunning and scientific deduction against the plotting of an avaricious, kill-crazy pillar of respectability who uses a fierce hound to slay his victims, is pictured in vivid style. The whole is soundly constructed mystery melodrama, a refreshing change from the round of mysteries that have featured slick, suave sleuths.

Like it or not, Basil Rathbone was Sherlock Holmes. The bar had been set and the public wanted more. The scriptwriters busily began exercising Fox's right to a follow-up movie – a new Holmes story – and Rathbone and Bruce were signed up to appear in *The Adventures of Sherlock Holmes*. The question was, could they follow up Conan Doyle's epic with what was, essentially, a concocted Holmes tale?

15

1940–1941

The Curious Case of
Ouida Rathbone

Born not from our flesh but born into our hearts. You were
longed for, wanted, and loved from the start.

Anon.

It seemed that as quickly as Basil earned his money, Ouida Rathbone
was planning how best to spend it. Given Basil's well-documented
dislike of parties and fuss, it seems that, rather than simply be
Mrs Rathbone and play the supportive wife, Ouida needed to be in
the spotlight in some form or another – and throwing lavish parties
for Hollywood A-listers was the perfect hobby for her and one way
of keeping her profile high.

Ouida's functions cost thousands of dollars and whatever she
did, there was no expense spared. For Rodion's wedding, she even
filled her swimming pool with orchids. Typical of her extravagance,
Hollywood columnist Ed Sullivan wrote the following in the spring
of 1939:

Arc lights, clusters of them, outlined the huge brown circus tent,
big enough for a Ringling Circus performance … Twin dance
floors occupied the main part of the tented interior… The acres

of tables started filling with formally dressed women and their escorts… Before the evening was over the caterers had served over eight hundred dinners.

It was incredible, but seemingly Basil was content to let his wife get on with it. He was too busy as one of the most bankable actors of the day and if Ouida was happy and distracted, it seems so was he – or perhaps he believed there was another, entirely different, distraction about to enter their lives that would give Ouida a new focus.

Just two weeks after *The Hound of the Baskervilles* was released, the Rathbones welcomed baby Cynthia into their lives. She was born on 13 April 1939, and within a few days was with Ouida and Basil, who had by then moved to a delightful mansion at 10728 Bellagio Road, Bel Air, California.

Cynthia was adopted as a newborn baby, but this, understandably, was largely kept private and never openly talked about. Indeed, many believe Cynthia never knew that Basil and Ouida were not her biological parents throughout her life. The adoption was the result of a number of miscarriages Ouida is believed to have had early in her marriage to Basil, and at 52 years of age it was a case of now or never in regard to raising a child.

One man who saw the Rathbones up close and personal – at least for a few weeks – was Joseph Ishikawa, who filled in as temporary help at the family home around the time of Cynthia's arrival. In 2014, he gave a brief, but fascinating, glimpse of the private life Ouida and Basil led in 1939.

He said:

Ouida Rathbone was considered the leading dinner hostess in Hollywood. One time, while I was working there, she had 100 guests to dinner. She had 12 stoves lined up along the walled fence over the golf course, each manned by a cook and each cooking from the same menu for one of ten tables each with 10 diners.

Of the two weeks I was on the job, Ouida also held a dinner party for 10 people which included Hedy Lamarr, Charles Boyer and his wife Pat, Norma Shearer the Canadian actress, Mervyn Leroy and his wife and several others.

I wasn't a professional butler and was just standing in for the usual houseboy who had injured his hand. I thought I would at least greet the guests at the door when they began arriving to save Ouida a job. As a courtesy and about two hours before dinner, a butler (French) showed up and very professionally took command while I assisted in the kitchen. I spoke to the butler in French, which impressed Ouida (eventually!). Norma Shearer had left her purse and I drove out to her house at Malibu Beach, but I left it with her doorman and never met her.

Evidently, the nisei whose place I took was only a Japanese houseboy, but he had comfortable quarters adjacent to the main house. Basil Rathbone was a very decent, considerate man. He didn't take a chauffeured limousine to work but drove himself, leaving at 6am and returning home after 6pm. One day he had spent 10 hours filming in the water and when he returned, he had a cheerful greeting for everyone. Then he asked Ouida how her day had gone. She had gotten up after noon and complained that the day had gone badly. He sympathized but she never inquired how his day had been.

I assumed a baby girl that was too young to crawl was Basil's and well taken care of by a trained nurse.

Cynthia brought much joy into Basil's life. For all the pain and hurt caused by his leaving Rodion behind with his first wife Marion, it seemed he wanted to make sure he got his second chance of fatherhood right. In his autobiography, Basil wrote:

As bald as a coot, she was a beautiful, healthy child, and her coming was a great compensation for our loss of Jack Miltern. How he would have loved her and how she would have loved him. They would have had much in common – a fierce independence and that Irish trait of needling a weak spot wherever they could find one.

Basil enjoyed a short break as a new father before filming commenced two months later on his second Holmes picture: *The Adventures of Sherlock Holmes*. This time he was given top billing and once again was joined by his close friend Nigel Bruce.

A strong cast included George Zucco and newcomer Ida Lupino in a story loosely based on the 1899 play written by William Gillette, rather than adapted from a Sir Arthur Conan Doyle book. Rathbone was on stellar form and given far more screen time than during his first outing as Holmes, with the fast-paced action allowing him to further develop the character, and even giving him the opportunity to display a vaudeville interpretation of 'I Do Like to be Beside the Seaside' during a brief disguised cameo role. This movie would be the first of his battles to outwit criminal mastermind Professor Moriarty, though Holmes's archenemy is wrestled off a rooftop and falls to his doom in one of the closing scenes – an indication that Fox weren't planning a lengthy run for The Great Detective.

Nigel Bruce wasn't overly impressed with what he thought was something of a rushed, muddled story, as he revealed:

On June 5th we commenced our second Sherlock Holmes picture, and once again my old friend Gene Markey was the producer. Besides Basil and myself, the cast included Ida Lupino .and complicated story which had no resemblance to any of the writings of Conan Doyle. In this picture Ida Lupino had her first dramatic part and making full use of her chances, she gave a grand performance which may be said to have started her on the road to stardom.

The film was released on 1 September and proved another box office success, along with a warm reception in Britain where the movie was released simply as *Sherlock Holmes*.

Copies of letters purported to be (and almost certainly) from Basil's hand suggest that the Rathbones' marriage may, at that stage, have been having difficulties, and that Ouida almost certainly suspected her husband was having an affair. The projection of a happy home seems anything but, with the content Basil wrote to a woman whose name will not be included in this book, due to a third-party promise not to offend or upset the family and descendants of the actress in question. Interestingly, it hints that Ouida may have been on medication or unwell at the time and that Nigel Bruce and his wife 'Bunny' were well aware of Basil's extramarital relationship – perhaps even conduits.

The first letter, written in 1940, reads:

Well darling …
I have finished a wonderful evening going around locking away all sharp objects and all the medications. It's 2.30am. Everyone is asleep. C was awake a while ago with a nightmare and soaking wet. We lost her rabbit (the little brown one) and I had to hunt him up before she would settle. She's fast asleep in my bed now. Such a small sad little thing she looks all curled up.

This is a kind of hell isn't it? Not sure how it's to be endured. God willing, we will find some way.

I'm so desperately sorry my darling [name removed] – for this awful wretchedness when your little cup is already so full. I can't bear to see you so pale and jumping at every little sound, and worst of all knowing I am only bringing more pain. Don't fret about me, all is quiet now, promise me you will eat & sleep. —

I'll call you but not tonight – reach me via the Bruces.

All my love is with you dearest girl

B

The mention of 'sharp objects and medications' infers that there were concerns for Ouida's mental health. Why else write such a sentence? It is possible Basil may have considered leaving Ouida around this period. Had he had enough of her free-spending and controlling nature and threatened as much? The note must have been written and hand-delivered, as the timing and mention of 'tonight' could only have had immediate relevance.

A second letter paints an ever more desperate situation for Basil and Ouida, who, it indicates, may have been heavily sedated:

> Darling – Cynthia woke up as I got home so I went to fetch her some water and while I was doing that Ouida came into the kitchen. I was prepared for the worst. But she was very quiet and calm. I made her some tea and took her back to bed because I didn't want her wandering the house alone, and I gave her a pill.
>
> I think she knows I was with you. If she had asked, I don't know what I would have said, but she didn't ask.
>
> She's sleeping peacefully. Everything is quiet. But I'm listening for every little sound, don't want to try and sleep, dreading she might wake up or something will happen. Everything hangs on such little threads. I'm praying, just praying this doesn't become something. She's been so much better – almost quite normal.
>
> I want so much to be able to talk to her and try to find some way – but I don't dare risk anything. She begs for the truth from all of us and we all smile and lie in our different ways because nothing else is possible now.
>
> I want to crawl back into your bed and never leave.
>
> – B

Whether the couple patched things up after this is not immediately clear. One school of thought is that Basil had pledged to look after Ouida, come what may, and felt he owed her for much of his success and that whatever he earned was due to her guidance. Is it possible that, when Ouida's health improved, Basil ended his affair with the mystery woman? Or did it continue? Whatever the truth, the Rathbones did not separate and besides, the Second World War had started in Europe and would become a major focus for both husband and wife, perhaps even bringing them closer together again.

Surprisingly, despite two solid Holmes successes at the box office, Twentieth Century Fox decided not to make any further Holmes movies, believing the character had limited appeal. It would prove to be a serious misjudgement by the studio bosses, and as a result it would be another three years before Rathbone once again donned his deerstalker.

The outbreak of war could have seriously affected Basil's career, and despite enormous success in the States he was prepared to risk everything and offer his services for king and country. Basil, now 47, wrote to the British armed forces – an incredibly selfless act for a man at the peak of his career, and who had witnessed the horrors of the First World War, more than two decades earlier, first-hand.

He later recalled:

War was declared in Europe in August 1939, and I wrote to the War Office in London offering my services. In due course I received an official letter of interminable length in reply. It began 'Dear Sir' and ended with 'Your obedient servant.' I waded through it and all it said was: 'You are too old!' Politely but firmly!

Nonetheless, he was determined to contribute and help his country in its hour of need. It is true he loved his life in America, its people and the freedom and the success it had brought him, but he still possessed the stout heart of a proud Englishman and remained fiercely loyal to his homeland.

Suspecting the conflict would escalate, he found it a difficult time to be away from England. He wrote:

Then came Dunkirk and Britain's year alone against the united Axis powers. It was then that Ouida organized her first benefit, the proceeds to be shared by the R. A. F. Benevolent Fund and the Red Cross. She organized it alone, with a secretary, at the Beverly Wilshire Hotel and netted some $10,000. It was a staggering job, attended by everyone who was anybody in the motion picture industry and was one of the most brilliant and beautiful and exciting functions I have ever attended.

By this time, I had been elected president of British War Relief on the Coast, a relief agency that had its headquarters in New York. This occupied much of my spare time of which I had all too little. Jules Stein of MCA Inc. had very wisely signed me up for five years with MGM. I also started in on the Sherlock Holmes pictures and the weekly radio series.

Indeed, it was a wise move by his agent, particularly securing radio work, with Rathbone's dulcet tones perfect for the medium. It also secured a guaranteed income at an unsettling time for the entertainment business. Nigel Bruce would later reveal that he was paid $500 per episode on radio, and it's safe to assume Rathbone earned double that – if so, it was the equivalent of approximately $18,000 per show and $750,000 per season in today's money.

Basil had already appeared many times in various radio shows during the 1930s, particularly on the Kraft Music Hall show hosted by Bing Crosby, where he made numerous guest appearances. He also appeared in radio dramas and panel shows that included a who's who of Hollywood superstars, with Cary Grant, Bette Davis, John Barrymore and The Marx Brothers among many, many others.

In the background, his war efforts continued.

He wrote:

We accepted this pattern of life, working quietly and carefully where and when we could. As president of British War Relief, I wrote to all the top executives of MGM asking them to contribute. Not one of them so much as answered my letters. But with the Warner Brothers it was very different.

They were terrific Anglophiles and supported us with both their time and money. Both Harry and Jack Warner were dedicated to our cause. One's major hope for results in making requests for help at this time was not to talk of Britain's problems and needs, but to use almost everyone's tremendous admiration for Winston Churchill as a means of approach.

Along with Nigel Bruce, Rathbone began recording *The Adventures of Sherlock Holmes* for New York's WJZ-NBC, and the weekly show proved extremely popular and ran for twenty-four weeks, covering many of Conan Doyle's classic Holmes adventures.

Far from his work drying up at a time of great uncertainty for the movie industry, he was arguably busier than ever, and his radio success had even further cemented him as the ultimate Sherlock Holmes in the public's opinion. He looked like Conan Doyle's super sleuth, he sounded as everyone imagined Holmes would sound and, in many ways, he inhabited the role perhaps all too easily.

Perhaps playing Holmes also helped him escape the villainous roles he had become famous for during the 1930s, and his first picture of 1940 was the delightful musical *Rhythm of the River*, alongside Bing Crosby and Mary Martin.

Crosby, an American superstar, was arguably at the peak of his powers and this was undoubtedly a vehicle aimed at his millions of adoring fans, but Rathbone is excellent in his comedic portrayal of successful composer Oliver Courtney. Music and comedy, this film was a joy for him to feature in, and the favourable reception placed the movie as one of Crosby's best for several years.

Among the many positive reviews, Bosley Crowther of the *New York Times* wrote, 'One of the most likeable musical pictures of the season', while *Photoplay* added: 'A comedy with music that has everything, plus a swell story that presents Bing Crosby and Mary Martin as a pair of song-writers who "ghost" for Basil Rathbone until they strike out on their own to find success. Top-notch songs and Oscar Levant's own special brand of comedy.'

His final movie of 1940 was another Darryl F. Zanuck production, *The Mark of Zorro*, which saw Basil return to his malevolent best as the scheming Captain Esteban Pasquale in a swashbuckler aimed at repeating the success of the Captain Blood and Robin Hood movies.

Tyrone Powers played the masked hero Zorro, while Rathbone was splendid as the former fencing instructor turned bad, and he revels in the superbly choreographed epic where he again gets to display his fencing prowess. The film was critically acclaimed and doubled its box office budget of $1 million, making a star out of Powers in the process.

Rathbone and Bruce then embarked on another epic second season of *Sherlock Holmes* for WJZ-NBC, with the twenty-four-week run lasting from October 1940 to March 1941, including a six-part version of *The Hound of the Baskervilles*. In two years, Rathbone had played Holmes fifty times – twice on the silver screen and forty-eight times on radio. It was an incredible run that was both lucrative and tiring, but it kept his star firmly towards the top of Hollywood's A-listers. The question was whether such a sustained spell of Holmes and Watson would prove creatively draining for Basil. Only time would tell.

16

1941–1944

Sherlock Takes Command

Work is the best antidote to sorrow, my dear Watson.

Sherlock Holmes

The February release of Basil's latest picture, *The Mad Doctor*, gave him another box office success as he played an Austrian physician who murders his unfaithful wife and then marries and murders a succession of wealthy women in his demented quest for inheritance.

It is fertile Rathbone territory, and his consistent run of top-notch performances saw him receive excellent reviews. The *Hollywood Reporter* called his performance 'stunning'.

Photoplay's review was equally fulsome in its praise:

Basil Rathbone is simply out of this world in his role of the mad doctor who marries 'em rich and leaves them – quite dead. He gets away with the murder business, too, until young John Howard comes along and suspects the worst when his own fiancée, Ellen Drew, falls under the doctor's spell. Brrrr, it gives us goose pimples just to write about it! And that Rathbone! But we did mention the beauty of his performance, didn't we?

Fellow cast member Martin Kosleck, who played Maurice Gretz, recalled his time on set with Basil, saying:

> I enjoyed working on *Mad Doctor* more than anything else in my career because of Basil Rathbone. He was a wonderful man… very precise… he rehearsed everything until it was perfect. Between scenes, we would walk around the Paramount lot and go over our lines… I loved that man.

Basil promoted the movie on *The Bob Hope Show* as demand for him as a guest reached an all-time high. He was the perfect interviewee: intelligent, witty and engaging, and enormously popular.

Comedy-horror flick *The Black Cat* followed, purportedly inspired by an Edgar Allan Poe short story – Poe was Hollywood's flavour of the month at that time – but it was largely disappointing considering its cast members. *Leonard Maltin's Movie Guide* described the picture thus: 'Hugh Herbert and Broderick Crawford get the laughs; others provide chills in a lively comedy-mystery not to be confused with the 1934 horror film. Look for Alan Ladd in a small role. Atmospheric photography by Stanley Cortez.'

Awarded 2.5 stars, it's a fair enough review. A rushed production of just two weeks hardly helped, with Basil appearing alongside Bela Lugosi for a second time, but a poor script and the ridiculous shooting schedule saw its release greeted with mixed to lukewarm reviews.

He then began filming *International Lady* from May to September, giving a typically strong performance described as such by the *Hollywood Reporter*: 'Basil Rathbone, in a sympathetic comedy role, gives a charming and amusing performance.'

There was no let-up for the prolific actor. *Paris Calling* would be Basil's last film of 1941 before he and Nigel Bruce returned for a lucrative third season of *Sherlock Holmes* on the radio. Once again, the weekly series ran from October to March, this time on WEAF-NBC, and consisted of twenty-two episodes, taking the series tally to sixty-eight to date.

Rathbone squeezed in a couple of movies early in 1942.

In February, he filmed *Crossroads* – and was back playing the villain to great effect – in a film that proved a surprisingly successful box office hit, grossing $2.3 million and making a profit of almost $750,000. Next up was the thriller *Fingers at the Window* early in the year – stealing the show as a demented serial killer who hypnotised other people to kill his victims, in what was only an average movie that would just about break even at the box office.

His war efforts with Ouida, toddler daughter Cynthia, radio slots and TV shows meant that he could barely stop to catch his breath. Rathbone must have despaired that he was back to only being seen as the bad guy, but the parts usually came with a healthy pay cheque and they were quick to turn around. And that year, Holmes would return to the movie theatres with Universal wisely deciding to take up the reins. Rathbone and Bruce had built up a large and loyal following on radio during their brief silver screen hiatus as Holmes and Watson, and the success of the first two films meant this was something of a no-brainer for studio executives.

Loosely based on Conan Doyle's 1917 story 'His Last Bow', the first decision Universal made was to bring Sherlock Holmes into the present day, explaining this at the start of *Sherlock Holmes and the Voice of Terror* with a disclaimer of sorts, suggesting Holmes was ageless and would solve crimes in any era. It read: 'Sherlock Holmes, the immortal character of fiction created by Sir Arthur Conan Doyle, is ageless, invincible and unchanging. In solving significant problems of the present day, he remains – as ever – the supreme master of deductive reasoning.'

There was a tongue-in-cheek reference to this at the start of the film where Holmes goes to grab his deerstalker and Watson urges him to take the fedora instead, which he does reluctantly. Aside from London being portrayed shrouded by peasouper fogs, the jump in time forty years or so was largely seamless. And it would be the first of many future time shifts for the dynamic duo.

With 'Scream Queen' Evelyn Ankers, star of a number of successful horror movies – most notably *The Wolf Man* – taking on the lead female role as 'Kitty', the film, soaked in the Nazi paranoia of the time, is an entertaining (if short – just 65 minutes!) return to the big screen for the faithful duo that ends, of course, with the Nazis' rear-ends well and truly spanked.

The brevity of the film was due to Universal's desire to make the Holmes franchise perfect for double features, with an hour or so the perfect length for the popular two-film double bills. It also kept the storylines fast paced and an easy watch for cinemagoers, but it meant they would largely be the supporting act for bigger movies.

The second Holmes film of the year was released on Christmas Day and proved to be another successful outing – *Sherlock Holmes and the Secret Weapon*. With Lionel Atwill taking on the role of Professor Moriarty (now risen from the grave, given his demise in *The Adventures of Sherlock Holmes*) and director Roy William Neill at the helm for the first of many Holmes pictures, *Secret Weapon* garnered favourable reviews, though it was Basil Rathbone, again enjoying the part of several disguised characters, who drove the narrative.

The *Hollywood Reporter* wrote: 'Basil Rathbone assumes the part of Sherlock Holmes with the suavity that is his stock in trade.'

Interestingly, reviewers and Sherlock Holmes aficionados often note that Nigel Bruce's Dr Watson is anything but the sharp, intuitive sidekick from the Conan Doyle books, but while Bruce portrays Watson as a lovable old grandfather, he has an undeniable charm and grace about him that is the perfect foil for his brilliant, analytical genius of a friend. Moreover, the public loved him.

Interestingly, despite appearances to the contrary, Bruce was three years younger than Basil Rathbone, and many fans came to love his portrayal of Dr Watson with his cheery outlook, total admiration for Holmes and that gruff yet gentle voice.

Basil managed to squeeze in one more movie towards the end of 1942, playing the lead alongside Joan Crawford in *Above Suspicion*, which held its own at the box office but received mixed reviews. Filming began in November and the movie was released early in the new year, but aside from a brief cameo as Holmes in *Crazy House*, there would be no further pictures that year, other than a couple more Holmes and Watson instalments.

Sherlock Holmes in Washington and *Sherlock Holmes Faces Death* undoubtedly kept the legion of Rathbone and Bruce fans happy. The pair continued to be something of a phenomenon off screen, too, with the *Sherlock Holmes* radio series kicking back into action on WOR-MBS and running over the next three years for almost 150 more episodes.

It's fair to say that Basil Rathbone and Nigel Bruce could play Holmes and Watson in their sleep, but Rathbone, with his creative spirit, was becoming heartily sick of playing the world's foremost detective.

He was in something of a creative vortex, and he had played the role so many times that, even after just five years of life as Sherlock Holmes, separating the character from the actor had become almost impossible. It was 1944 and he was contracted to make several more Holmes pictures, but given the opportunity he would have hung up his deerstalker for the final time and never visited 221B Baker Street again.

17

1944–1945

A Case of Lost Identity

You can't have employment and despise employers ... No goose, no golden eggs.

Paul Tsongas

Basil Rathbone and Nigel Bruce's prolific Holmes and Watson portrayals showed no signs of ending anytime soon. *The Spider Woman* was the seventh movie the pair had starred in and was released in January 1944, pleasing the series' loyal followers and ensuring there was plenty more gas in the tank for Conan Doyle's creation.

A favourite of many Holmes enthusiasts, AllMovies.com describes it as:

Filled to overflowing with amusing dialogue and devilishly clever plot twists (one of them involving an autistic pygmy!), *Sherlock Holmes and the Spider Woman* is among the best of the Universal Holmes series. The best bit? Told to 'act inconspicuous', Inspector Lestrade (Dennis Hoey) ceremoniously rolls his eyes upward and begins whistling loudly – whereupon Dr Watson chides him with 'Inconspicuous, Lestrade, not half-witted.'

The series was gathering momentum, and indeed, the May 1944 release of *The Scarlet Claw* suggested, if anything, the films were getting better. If Rathbone and Bruce really were going through the motions mentally and professionally, it never showed, with the eighth instalment considered one their best pictures to date. Well-crafted and suitably creepy, the film shifts Holmes and Watson to Canada, and the rural gloom and rolling fog put many in mind of *The Hound of the Baskervilles*.

The *Showman's Trade Review* reported:

> Basil Rathbone and Nigel Bruce have fallen into the characters of Sherlock Holmes and Dr Watson so perfectly that one no longer thinks in terms of a good acting role well done. They are the characters to the life. The excellence of their work should not distract from the fact that Roy William Neill, who produced, directed and joined in the writing of the screenplay, has almost fallen into the part which traditionally goes to A. Conan Doyle, author of the famous tales. Sell this newest of the series like its predecessors. The theme of occult phenomena is a good one to rig up a debate between spiritualists and those who deny its existence. Such a debate will attract many people and would be worth the small loss of time from your continuous run.

Motion Picture Daily added:

> In *The Scarlet Claw*, Sherlock Holmes, played by Basil Rathbone, and Dr Watson, portrayed by Nigel Bruce, carry on the famous Sir Arthur Conan Doyle characters with the deft touch. Aided by chilling fog on the marshlands, a well-planted fear of the mysterious 'monsters' among the villagers, the mystery builds suspense, capped by action, and touches of Dr Watson's stuffy, whimsical humour in just the right dosages.

While the reviews were good and the box office steady, there was no reason for Universal to pull the plug on this incredibly popular movie franchise.

Nonetheless, there would be a welcome break from the series for Basil, who had been cast as George Adams in the Red Skelton and Esther Williams vehicle *Bathing Beauty*. With delightful songs and settings, and a stunning swimming pool scene that reportedly cost $250,000, it was a million miles away from the crime capers and analytical world of Sherlock Holmes. Though the part is relatively undemanding, Basil's love of music and the mood shift of this light-hearted musical made it a box office smash – the biggest Basil had been involved with yet – yielding almost $7 million in worldwide receipts and making MGM more than $4.5 million in profits.

It was a much-needed change for Basil, but he was soon back on the case in *The Pearl of Death* which was released in August 1944 – the third Holmes picture of the year. And a month later, both Rathbone and Bruce were on the silver screen again – but this time in the costume drama *Frenchman's Creek*. Based on the Daphne du Maurier bestseller set in Cornwall, and starting Joan Fontaine (sister of Olivia de Havilland, who had played alongside Rathbone and Errol Flynn in the swashbuckling Captain Blood and Robin Hood pictures), the movie was only a moderate success, receiving largely lukewarm reviews.

In retrospect, the timing and casting of the movie was not perhaps the wisest decision Basil would ever make. Considering their long partnership, putting Rathbone and Bruce in a costume drama inevitably made cinemagoers think Holmes and Watson were making an appearance – albeit in costume – rather than the actors as individuals having a creative existence outside those characters.

Away from filming, Basil and Ouida continued with their considerable war efforts, organising fundraisers and hosting charity balls while also being parents to Cynthia, who was closest to her father, who was attentive and enjoyed the company of his small daughter.

He wrote of the time:

Meanwhile I played golf, went to the races at Santa Anita, worked in the garden and attended to one's picture making and radio work. Cynthia was growing into a beautiful child, with a mass of blond curls and a strong personality. I shall never forget the day when Cynthia's governess came blazing into our bedroom saying the child was an 'ungovernable little brat,' and she and Ouida had a tremendous blow-up. As the storm reached its zenith, I felt a little hand take hold of mine and squeeze it. I looked down into Cynthia's sparkling excited eyes. Then I heard her whisper, 'Oh Dadda, how I love trouble!' She would have been about five years old at the time, and was attending kindergarten at Marymount Catholic School, a short walk across the Bel Air golf course. On the governess's day off I would sometimes go and pick her up and walk her home across the golf course with her friends the McAllister boys. One day we were walking back, and the McAllister boys and she were playing tag. They were running and shouting and laughing when suddenly Cynthia hauled off and hit the younger boy a terrific 'haymaker!' I was quickly between them, fearing the boy might retaliate. I pointed out to Cynthia it was a disgraceful thing to have done as the little boy was also a little gentleman (something I was none too sure of at the moment!) and couldn't hit her back. Well, that put an end to that. But I was curious to know why she had hit him so violently. So when I got her alone I asked her, and she told me that he sat directly behind her in school and rubbed chewing gum into her hair! It was all I could do not to laugh. We didn't have chewing gum when I was a kid, but if we had, it would have been a wonderful idea and I know I'd have tried it. It is perhaps the fact that I have always been able to look back at myself as a child and share some of Cynthia's childish vagaries with her that has helped us to have such confidence in one another.

Moving into 1945, the exhaustive *Sherlock Holmes* radio series would run until May, having appeared weekly for two long years, though Basil enjoyed the radio series where he believed people's imaginations could run riot, giving the Holmes stories an added dimension.

He wrote:

Radio is unquestionably a superior medium to television because it makes us use our imaginations. I have been told by literally hundreds of people that when we were doing the *Sherlock*

Holmes series, they would turn out the lights or if they had a fire sit round it and let their imaginations go fancy free. Many have told me that the hound in *The Baskervilles* was far more frightening to them on radio than it could ever be on the screen or their television sets. In the days of radio, of The Theatre Guild of the Air be it here said that their program was ever striving for quality, intelligence, and good taste. I have played many times for them and every time I was invited it was a worth-while experience. And also, it must be said that in the theatre the Theatre Guild has been an outstanding leader for over forty years. Their record I think is unique in the annals of the American theatre. I doubt that we shall see their like again.

That year, 1945, would see three more Sherlock Holmes films. *The House of Fear* was released in March, *The Woman in Green* in July and *Pursuit to Algiers* hit the screens in October, by which time the Second World War had finally ended.

The House of Fear was another polished effort from Universal, returning to the Victorian values of Holmes and away from the 'Nazis' attempt to take over the planet' themes that had worn a little thin in Hollywood. Set in a creepy house in a remote Scottish village, it is similar to the 1939 Agatha Christie novel *Ten Little Indians*.

Holmes, thankfully, has returned to his debonair slicked-back hair, after a couple of outings where he sported a bizarre combed forward windswept style in the previous few movies. The plot concerns a secretive group of men known as the Good Comrades, who are disappearing one by one. It is loosely based on Conan Doyle's 'The Adventure of the Five Orange Pips'.

Suspicious locals, bodysnatching, thunderstorms and shadowy figures: it is quintessential Holmes, and a satisfying picture that received surprisingly average reviews. *Showman's Trade Review* reported:

Again, Sherlock Holmes goes forth to solve a mystery that hasn't much suspense but an over-abundance of killings. It's the kind of a picture that should make a satisfactory program offering in situations where patrons aren't too critical. For armchair detectives there's a challenge in the solution, for the story has a surprise ending. Basil Rathbone and Nigel Bruce are very satisfactory in the roles of the famous detective and his assistant, respectively. Others in the cast whose appearances are worthy of mention are Sally Shepherd, Paul Cavanagh and Aubrey Mather. Roy William Neill produced and directed.

Was Hollywood finally tiring of Holmes and Watson?

Whether it was or not, there was clearly still a hunger for the series, and besides, with the tastier roles increasingly hard to find for Basil by the mid-1940s, Holmes kept the Rathbones in the comfort they had become accustomed to – and Basil still had a lot of extravagant parties to pay for with Ouida's reputation as the Queen of Hollywood showing no signs of ending any time soon.

Interestingly, the $192,000 budget for *House of Fear* revealed that Basil was paid $20,000 – about $275,000 in today's money – and Nigel Bruce $12,000. And as this was the tenth Holmes picture made, Basil was comfortably a millionaire in today's money.

The summer release of *The Woman in Green* was followed by *Pursuit to Algiers* in the autumn, which many fans feel was perhaps the weakest yet of the Holmes and Watson adventures. At best, it is standard fare and perhaps the inevitable result of a rapidly tiring franchise. Basil revealed some interesting production secrets in a university lecture, with the short turnaround and camaraderie perhaps standing out more than anything.

He revealed:

None of those pictures made at Universal took more than 17 days. We never started shooting before nine – today it's 8:30 or even 8 o'clock – and worked until six. No night work unless required by the script. At four o'clock there was half an hour for tea. This mood – the whole of the making of the pictures – they had a sense of 'family.' We all got along very well together. We had our little differences from time to time but the one lovely character of them all was our dear friend, the director.

We loved Roy Neill. He was mousy, a little guy. A little guy and as sweet as they come. But a damn good disciplinarian. We didn't disobey orders on the set. We were always on time and we always knew our lines. It was thoroughly professional.

Poignant words for the British-born producer-director, considering what lay ahead in 1946 for both Neill and Sherlock Holmes ...

18

1946

The Curse of Sherlock Holmes

Sir Arthur felt at one time that he had created a sort of Frankenstein that he could not escape from. And so, he decided to kill Mr Sherlock Holmes …

Basil Rathbone

The following year, 1946, would be a year when everything would change for Basil Rathbone and Nigel Bruce.

Basil was desperate to escape the world of Sherlock Holmes and Hollywood, and the decisions he would make would put a strain on his close friendship with Nigel Bruce.

It began with the release of *Terror by Night*, which hit the cinemas on 1 February and was regarded as neither the worst nor the best Holmes picture. Bosley Crowther of the *New York Times* wrote: 'This episode in the famous detective's career is told in a tight continuity and with flavoursome atmosphere … Mr Rathbone is silky smooth as usual.'

It was the thirteenth Sherlock Holmes picture and would prove to be the penultimate appearance of the dynamic duo – at least as far as these two cherished English actors were concerned. At sixty minutes, this episode was also the shortest, edited to fit in on double bills or as an opening feature for a bigger movie.

Dressed to Kill (released as *Sherlock Holmes and the Secret Code*) was filmed in the spring of 1946 and released in May. Again, it kept an army of Holmes fans happy, and again, Rathbone and Bruce did their jobs professionally with no hint of the tedium Rathbone was now feeling.

At that stage, though there was no hint it would be the final instalment from Universal, it seemed the franchise had finally run its course. In simple terms, Rathbone had had enough and wanted out. With his filming commitments and contracts honoured, he decided he'd had his fill of Hollywood life and decided to move back to New York where he could once again pursue his first love, the theatre.

By all accounts, Ouida was reluctant to leave California, but reluctantly accepted her husband was hellbent on quitting the life they had led. He was mentally and creatively burned out and, at the very least, needed a lengthy break away from being the world's smartest detective. When he announced his intentions, it put a huge strain on his friendship with Nigel Bruce, who had made Dr Watson his own and, in the process, had also boxed himself into a creative corner from which it would be hard to escape. Moreover, the affable Bruce had thoroughly enjoyed playing Dr Watson and believed the series still had plenty of life left in it.

But for Basil Rathbone, playing Sherlock Holmes had made his public life torturous. In fact, his recollections of life after Holmes show his frustration and are, for such a brilliant actor, quite sad in many ways.

He later wrote:

'Hi there, Sherlock – how's Dr Watson?' This greeting might quite easily prove to be my epitaph, if not in substance at least in effect. It is a greeting that in most cases I have not welcomed, for in general it has carried with it the connotation 'We too are amused and entertained by your little game of sleuthing, how goes it, pal?' I do not remember a single instance from 1939 to 1962 where an interviewer from some newspaper or magazine, or a member of an audience, or a friend has not smiled somewhat indulgently when the subject of my association with Mr Sherlock Holmes has arisen.

In the upper echelon of my very considerable following as Mr Holmes, there has always been a somewhat patronizing, if polite, recognition of my modest achievement. In the lower echelon I have experienced nothing but embarrassment in the familiar street-comer greeting of recognition, which is inevitably followed by horrendous imitations of my speech, loud laughter, and ridiculing quotes of famous lines such as 'Quick, Watson, the needle' or 'Elementary, my dear Watson,' followed by more laughter at my obvious discomfort. Quite frankly and realistically, over the years the most famous fictional characters in all literature has not received that respectful recognition to which I feel Sir Arthur Conan Doyle's masterpieces entitle him. Has it been my fault? I do not think so. And certainly, it is not the fault of those who were responsible for producing 14 pictures and some two hundred weekly radio broadcasts between 1939 and 1946. Professionally it has always been conceded that both pictures and broadcasts were of an exceptionally high quality. Could it be that our efforts somewhat resembled museum pieces? Here possibly may be a clue to the problem.

The problem was Rathbone was instantly recognisable – he looked in real life exactly as he did in the Holmes movies. Unless he went out in disguise or avoided public places, he was stuck with Sherlock Holmes for life.Yes, it had given him great wealth and made him even more famous around the world, but he took no comfort from it and it remained to be seen what effect it would have on his career going forward.At 54, he was still in his prime and desperate to explore new avenues – the question was, would studios give him that opportunity?

Despite there being no new instalments scheduled, It seemed there would be an open door at Universal for Sherlock Holmes, should he ever reconsider. But that door not so much slammed shut as creaked closed, and became even less likely when the director of the last twelve Holmes adventures died suddenly. Roy William Neill was just 59 years old when he died of a heart attack in London in December. It was a crushing loss for both Basil and Nigel Bruce.

Interestingly, Neill had been considering shooting one or two Holmes pictures in England, and this might have led to Basil reconsidering his decision – but that idea died along with Neill and never surfaced again.

Basil revealed more of his professional plight in his auto-biography, writing:

> I was also deeply concerned with the problem of being 'typed,' more completely 'typed' than any other classic actor has ever been or ever will be again. My fifty-two roles in twenty-three plays of Shakespeare, my years in the London and New York theatre, my scores of motion pictures, including my two Academy Award nominations, were slowly but surely sinking into oblivion: and there was nothing I could do about it, except to stop playing Mr Holmes, which I could not do owing to the existence of a long-term contract. I sincerely hope that this objective and unprejudiced analysis of a problem I had had to live with for so many years may not offend those who are still truly dedicated Sherlockians, many of whom are close personal friends of mine and have unquestionably been not only entertained, but have found our performances in these pictures and broadcasts rewarding.

He admitted he found himself in a similar position to that which Sir Arthur Conan Doyle had, adding:

> In John Dickson Carr's excellent biography of Sir Arthur Conan Doyle, he relates that Sir Arthur felt at one time that he had created a sort of Frankenstein that he could not escape from. And so he decided to kill Mr Sherlock Holmes at the Reichenbach Falls and be done with him. Public outrage at this callous murder of Mr Holmes by Sir Arthur was so great that Sir Arthur was literally forced to bring him back from the dead and for a while my

long-time friendship with Nigel Bruce suffered severe and recurring shocks. The Music Corporation of America, who represented me at that time, treated me as if I were 'sick-sick-sick.'

Despite this, MCA would call Basil – who, by that point, had sold his home in Bel Air and returned to New York – and inform him a new, lucrative seven-year deal had been agreed in principle for more Sherlock Holmes adventures on the radio. It was an offer that would ensure both Rathbone and Bruce security as they approached their 60s, but Basil emphatically turned the offer down. He'd had enough and that was the end of the matter, and he informed MCA in no uncertain terms not to raise the topic again.

For Nigel Bruce, however, it was the end of an era. Loveable on screen and in real life, this devoted family man had created one of the silver screen's most enduring characters. He was the perfect foil for Rathbone and though their friendship would recover, Bruce's career would not.

Bruce had decided to persevere with Dr Watson for another season of radio productions. Elizabeth McLeod, writing for Radio Classics, penned 'America's Favourite Englishman' and recalled how Bruce's initial desire to continue the role soon turned sour for him. She wrote:

> Nigel Bruce elected to continue for another season, and for his trouble received star billing and a substantial raise. Actor Tom Conway came aboard to replace Rathbone as Holmes when the series resumed for the fall season.
>
> All was not pleasant behind the scenes, with the series writing staff constantly at odds with the producer. Tensions ripped at the program throughout that season, and Bruce no longer found the experience enjoyable. At the end of the season, he gave his last performance as Watson, and an era came to its finish.

It just wasn't the same without Basil Rathbone. He would go on to play one or two eccentric cameos here and there before the work began to steadily dry up. Unlike Basil, he wasn't a classical actor who could return to the stage and try his hand elsewhere, and though playing Dr Watson had undoubtedly brought him great wealth and fame, it was he who would perhaps suffer even more from the curse of Sherlock Holmes.

19

1946–1951

Lost in New York

Movies will make you famous; Television will make you rich;
But theatre will make you good.

Terence Mann

Basil Rathbone was no fool and would have known there could be difficulties ahead, but even he must have been surprised at the lack of offers after returning to New York. He wasn't interested in radio and wanted a break from making pictures, but the flood of work for such a major movie star open to offers simply didn't materialise.

It quickly became clear that Basil's portrayal of Sherlock Holmes was a major concern to prospective employers, who were worried that casting him would harm their production – the fact was, prising apart the actor and the character he'd played was something casting directors and producers weren't prepared to gamble on.

It was the beginning of a slow and demoralising decline for one of the greatest actors Britain had produced, but he was back in Manhattan, close to Broadway again and the buzz and energy of Broadway, and immediately felt better for it. Explaining his reasons for leaving California, he wrote:

It wasn't instinct, (or was it perhaps?) but just luck that we decided to return to New York in June of 1946. Most of our friends considered us mad and pleaded with us not to throw away my career and our home. However, there were many contributing factors that influenced this move at this time.

Los Angeles had become a very cosmopolitan city during the war, and our war work had been most stimulating to us both. Without it, and no longer meeting continuously with interesting people from all over the world, we felt the community would slip back into a conventional pattern that might prove to be a tremendous let down. Also, we felt I had accomplished as much as was coming to me in motion pictures at this time, and that I needed another springboard in order to return successfully. I had had seven years of Sherlock Holmes and was not only tired and bored with the series but felt myself losing ground in other fields of endeavour. And last but not least I was literally aching to get back to my first love, the theatre.

Returning to the stage made perfect sense, but he needed a meaty part to get him back on track and help people remember that he was an actor who had first made his name on the stage and only later starred in some of the biggest successes Hollywood had seen for more than a decade. It was a challenge, but one he threw himself into wholeheartedly, as he done with everything he attempted in his life.

The motion picture industry imploded in the next few years after Basil left California, so the move east was not the worst decision in the world, but the turning down of the long radio contract MCA had negotiated for him to return as Holmes was perhaps not the wisest idea. Of course, he had no idea what lay ahead at the time and it was a brave decision – he simply had to make his move back to the theatre work to justify the loss of hundreds of thousands of dollars.

Meanwhile, Ouida updated an old play called *Jealousy* and renamed it *Obsession*, and this would be the vehicle the Rathbones hoped would provide that early success. They took the play on the road, and initially it was warmly received as it started on the West Coast to packed houses, before losing some momentum in the Midwest. By the time it arrived in New York, the early verve and optimism had evaporated and it ran for just three weeks at the Plymouth Theatre before closing down. It was a blow, but a defeat on points rather than a clean knockout – that would come later.

The Rathbones moved into an apartment at 10 Gracie Square in Manhattan, overlooking the East River, while their landlord became their tenant, taking on their home in Bel Air before eventually purchasing it. It was a mutually beneficial agreement that effectively meant they could live rent-free for a year with an option to buy. They quickly settled back to life in Manhattan, but the New York that Basil had left behind was very different to the one he now found himself in.

He recalled:

> Only one thing troubled me. I could not find a play or anyone willing to consider me for one. One well-known author came to see me. I wanted to do his play about King David, and there was no question that he wanted me. But both he and the producer decided against me because of my seven years' identification with Sherlock Holmes. They felt this identification would be a hazard to them. So, during the season of 1946–47 I did nothing but guest spots on radio, not one of them worth mentioning.

The curse of Sherlock Holmes, indeed.

At least when he had become typecast as a villain, there was always another role waiting in the wings, but the Sherlock Holmes problem was much bigger than he had first feared. It was going to take a long time for him to be free of Sherlock, and he suspected there was the very real threat that he might never be. For the first time since arriving in America, he had endured something of a lean year, and the longer he was out of pictures, the less likely his chances of landing leading roles became. Had the gamble failed miserably?

The Rathbones rented a vacation home in Sharon, Connecticut, overlooking the Berkshire Hills, having decided not to purchase the apartment at Gracie Square, though after the sale of their Bel Air home they did purchase a house at 9 East 92nd Street in Manhattan, overlooking Central Park. Then came the break he had been hoping for.

In the spring of 1947, Basil received an offer from Jed Harris to appear in a new play, *The Heiress*. Harris was adamant only Basil Rathbone could play the role of Dr Sloper, and though Ouida thought it was a bad move, it would prove to be anything but. Harris was a man on a mission, and after securing finance, was meticulous in his preparation for the play. His hard work paid off.

The Heiress was a resounding success. It was an instant hit and played in New York for a year before setting out on tour for another year, playing to packed houses across the States and running for 410 performances until September 1949. It also earned Basil his first Tony Award for a lead actor in a play – his first win after previously being nominated for *Romeo and Juliet*. The success of *The Heiress* both at the theatre box office and personally for Basil, who had once again shown his versatility as an actor, had come at a crucial time in his professional career. Quitting Hollywood had been a huge gamble, but it had finally paid off and also given him something that had been absent for so long: creative fulfilment. He'd taken on a role that Ouida didn't feel was right and created a character that was different from anything he'd done before, yet it had proved to be a masterstroke.

While *The Heiress* had been performing, he had also recorded a forty-four-week radio drama, *The Tales of Fatima*, for CBS. A mystery show, starring Rathbone as various characters, it ran from January until October 1949 and came with a healthy pay cheque.

The question was, what was next? Had he done enough to convince directors and producers that he could successfully play characters other than Sherlock Holmes and, more importantly, entertain the paying public? The one concern was that the theatre was somewhat limited and played to a small proportion of the general populace. Though he may have proved a point to theatregoers, he hadn't appeared in a movie for almost two years and in Hollywood, out of sight is very much out of mind. There were no offers of any substance on the table, and the stark reality was that studios felt that offering him a part was still a major gamble. While *The Heiress* had undoubtedly proved a point and the Tony Award had given him tremendous satisfaction, his movie career had virtually come to a standstill. Aged 57, the days of romantic leads were long gone and even the endless offers to play cunning villains, despots and scoundrels had completely dried up.

The Rathbones moved to a more manageable apartment in the fall of 1950, selling their 9 East 92nd home and moving a block or two further up. Though there was no indication that the sale was due to financial difficulties, Ouida's continued taste for a lavish life-style had undoubtedly put a strain on their finances. At least Basil had repaired his friendship with Nigel Bruce, who had remained in California with his family where he was a leading light in the size-able expat community, but Bruce had rarely worked since *Sherlock Holmes*. It was heart-breaking for both men, particularly as they had given many millions so much pleasure.

The Heiress had scratched an itch, but it wasn't enough. Reluctantly, in 1951, Basil and Ouida decided there was only one thing to do. It was time for him to once again don the deerstalker, smoke the pipe and occasionally play the violin. But it was a move that would go disastrously wrong ...

1951–1953

A Fall from Grace

'All the world's a stage, and all the men and women merely players; they have their exits and their entrances, and one man in his time plays many parts.'

William Shakespeare

By late 1951, Basil Rathbone had finally accepted that his Hollywood days were over. The Tony Award sat gathering dust on his mantlepiece and hadn't brought the flood of interesting theatre opportunities it deserved. He appeared briefly in one or two plays, with *The Gioconda Smile* the most successful, running for forty-one performances in New York followed by a short tour.

There were occasional radio shows, appearances as a guest panellist here and there and increasing TV show guest spots, including several on Milton Berle and Frank Sinatra shows. He also recorded a pilot TV episode for *Sherlock Holmes* for NBC, but tellingly it wasn't taken up for syndication by any networks and didn't develop into a series.

If the public and studios couldn't see him as anyone but Sherlock Holmes, then perhaps it was time to accept defeat and give them what they wanted – if it wasn't too late. Convinced this was perhaps now the only route back towards his former glories, this would be the way forward for Rathbone. But with studio bosses focusing increasingly on science fiction and little green men from Mars, the seemingly dated plots and characters of Sir Arthur Conan Doyle's yarns were now off the menu. The only alternative was to bring Holmes to the theatre. It seemed a natural progression, with legions of fans of the Great Detective still out there, and would couple his most famous creation with the environment he enjoyed the best.

Stan Laurel, writing in 1952, highlighted the plight of many of the 1930s movie and theatre stars at the time when he wrote:

> Regarding artistes dropping films for night clubs, in most cases, I think it's due to circumstances, there are many times when there is a slump in picture production, so during these periods, the actors try to keep busy in other mediums such as clubs, TV or theatre shows instead of being idle and waiting around. Some, of course, who have a name and have the necessary talent for night clubs, can command a great deal of money, especially in Las Vegas where they can – and do – pay $20,000 to $50,000 a week – those are star names and have box office attraction of course, so it isn't a matter of testing their popularity. Basil Rathbone is originally a stage actor and many like him prefer to do a show on Broadway or on the road because it's a change of atmosphere and they like to feel the immediate reaction of an audience. On the other hand, there are many who can't get work anymore in the films and have to resort to anything they can get, even to doing commercials and suchlike on TV.

Basil convinced Ouida to write a new play, inspired by the stories of Sir Arthur Conan Doyle, and began plans for a theatre run. Sadly, he would have to proceed without his close friend and co-star Nigel Bruce, who had suffered a heart attack. It was almost unthinkable that Rathbone and Bruce would not play the intrepid duo together, and perhaps underlined how important Bruce's bumbling Dr Watson had been in the success of their fourteen movies together.

Though Rathbone and Bruce repaired their friendship, it had been a painful parting and undoubtedly affected Bruce's health in the years that followed. He almost certainly would have jumped at the chance to join Holmes in more adventures on stage, but his health simply wouldn't allow it.

Basil had become convinced there was life left in Holmes from the reaction of the fans he met on the *Evening with Basil Rathbone* tour he had developed. During his informal one-man show, he shared show-business stories, gave Shakespearian readings and took questions from the audience. Holmes was never far from the topic of conversation, which had encouraged him to explore the opportunities of reviving the role.

He wrote:

I had been away from Mr Holmes for approximately five years and felt I might risk a renewal of my acquaintance with him. Ouida read all *The Adventures* very carefully, making copious notes. After some months she came up with what seemed a masterly construction, using material from five of the Conan Doyle stories. I was immensely intrigued. We did a lot of thinking and talking and discussing. It looked like a 'sure fire' success, especially since I was still closely identified with the character of Sherlock Holmes, by which name I was still more often than not greeted by strangers almost everywhere I went.

I was trying out my *Evening with Basil Rathbone* around the country and to be O.K.'d by the Conan Doyle estate, Ouida had stayed closely to legitimate Sherlockiana. Wherever she could she used the original dialogue, borrowed from any and all of 'the adventures', and where this was not possible had written a most excellent facsimile thereof. It was a workmanlike job, and most faithful to the traditions that made these stories classics. Mr Adrian Conan Doyle came to New York (the executor of his father's estate) on private business. We met with him and his charming Dutch wife and found them both most enthusiastic about the play. Adrian told us he was sure it would have his father's blessing.

With the play complete, the Rathbones sent out the script to a number of New York theatre managers, but were disappointed by the lukewarm response. Some gave constructive advice and suggested changes, many of which Ouida incorporated into the rewrites. But throughout 1952 the play still hadn't been taken up, until early in 1953 a press agent turned producer, Bill Doll, took the plunge enthusiastically, and after agreeing to share the productions costs, both Doll and investor friends of the Rathbones coughed up a hefty $50,000 to bring the play to the stage.

Everyone connected was convinced it had all the necessary ingredients to become a huge success, and rehearsals began. The initial reticence towards the project didn't worry Basil – he had been part of enough huge theatrical successes to know that many of the greatest Broadway shows had endured similar troubled beginnings.

He wrote:

Stewart Chaney was engaged to design the sets and costumes, Reginald Denham to direct. Our cast included Thomas Gomez as Moriarty, Madame Novotna as Irene Adler and Jack Rains as Watson (my good friend Nigel Bruce had suffered a serious heart attack and was unable to join us). We rehearsed for three weeks in New York and then went to Boston for a three-week try-out before coming back to New York.

The first warning that all was not well came when I went down to the Shubert Theatre in Boston on the Monday morning to unpack. I had walked my dog Ginger across Boston's Common. (Ouida and Ginger and I were staying at the Ritz, one of the most charming and civilized hotels in America.) There was no line-up at the box office, only desultory buying.

We would open slowly, it seemed. Everyone in the front of the house wore masks and spoke hesitantly as to our prospects! Of course, the reviews would help a great deal, and the local chapter of 'The Baker Street Irregulars' were with us to a man.

The first dress rehearsal at the Shubert Theatre on the Monday night was catastrophic. Everything went wrong, including the stage manager, who fainted at his desk from a mild heart attack. Even the prospects of sabotage occurred to us. But by whom? Edgar Allan Poe's ghost? We returned to our hotel at 4 A.M. in the morning, worn-out and deeply concerned and depressed. At the next night's dress rehearsal things went a little better after a hard day's work on technical problems. But tempers were frayed, and everyone was passing the buck. It was the most incompetent stage crew I have ever worked with. The fact that the sets, beautifully designed, proved to be impractical did not help, and tired actors, including myself, started to muff their lines. So many high hopes were bending perilously before the blast, while the ugly spectre of failure lurked in dark corners.

The exhaustive process of bringing Holmes to the stage would also be its undoing.

Mentally and physically tired, Basil gave what he described as a 'mechanical performance' and fluffed his lines in the first scene, never quite recovering thereafter. The pressures of producing and carrying the play had fallen squarely on his shoulders, and whereas it had always been the responsibility of others if a play was a success or bombed, this time Basil Rathbone's career – and financial stability – hung on this production being a success.

Surprisingly, he clearly still had the respect of and held some credit with the critics, with the reviews nowhere near as bad as he and Ouida had feared – the play clearly needed work, but there was hope. Or so it seemed. On the nights that followed, the theatre played to half-empty houses or sometimes much worse. Business was bad and it had been the worst possible try-out for the opening night in New York, where events quickly concluded.

He wrote:

It was a Tuesday night and Wednesday was a matinee. As Ouida and I went home we avoided the obvious. But I imagine we were both prepared for the worst. Business in Boston had been bad – very bad. Even the reviews had not helped us much. The opening night audience in New York had seemed listless and only modest applause had greeted our efforts. The Wednesday morning reviews dug a deep grave for us. The afternoon papers shovelled us in, and in due course the magazines covered us up.

After just three performances, Sherlock Holmes's theatrical life had ended. It was a disaster for Basil who, in hindsight, realised the whole project had been doomed to failure. He added:

How could so many intelligent professional people have been so hopelessly mistaken? For myself be it said that, like Conan Doyle at the end of the first *Adventures*, try as I would my heart was not really in it. I hoped to be carried by the volume of public opinion that had supported me so enthusiastically from 1939 to 1946. But this was 1953. Seven years had passed – yes, we were at least seven years too late! I believe it possible that had I returned to New York from the West Coast in this play in 1947 the results might have been very different. Then there was this new gadget television that was sweeping the country with one-hour and half-hour plays.

We were outdated, hopelessly outdated. In Boston I had noticed there were rarely ever any young people in our audiences. I should estimate the average age at well over thirty. That meant that nearly fifty per cent of our potential audience were not interested.

As if his spirit at that point couldn't have been lower, the tragic news that Nigel Bruce had died in October 1953 of heart failure left Basil and Ouida heartbroken. He was just 58 years old and though they lived on opposite sides of the United States, Basil knew he would miss his old friend forever. Sherlock Holmes was over, and it was the passage of time that had finally done what Moriarty and Conan Doyle had failed to do. Dr Watson had been taken too soon, Holmes director Roy Neill had also passed away, and the flickering embers of a magnificent acting career appeared to be steadily going out. That would probably have been true for any other actor – but this was Basil Rathbone and he was determined to give the fires one final stoking ...

21

1953–1960

The Admirable Mr Rathbone

The measure of intelligence is the ability to change.

Albert Einstein

Basil Rathbone's decline as a bankable movie star and the crushing failure of Sherlock Holmes at the theatre left him at a career low point going into 1954, but he wasn't about to give up the ghost and feel sorry for himself. Throughout his life he'd overcome adversity, dug his heels in when necessary, and more often than not survived and prospered.

He was well aware that the professional life he'd led for more than twenty years was going to have to change, but his career was far from over. There might be fewer movie roles to be had, but the ones that came his way would all be considered. He was astute and knew there was still plenty of work to be had, even if it occasionally meant poking fun at himself every now and then. He embraced TV more than ever, and continued to be a regular and popular guest on a number of shows, and an in-demand panellist on game shows such as *The Name's the Same*. He also held variety spots on Perry Como's and Milton Berle's shows, among many others, where his sharp wit and intelligence shone through.

They were light and easy performances for a man now in his 60s and he was a charming and engaging guest. He'd occasionally ham it up with the host if need be and wasn't afraid to make fun of himself. There was no pressure to attract an audience or have studios bank on his name to ensure box office success and he appeared to be at ease with the medium, even if his heart lay elsewhere.

He wrote for TV and admitted being well paid for his trouble, and appeared in a number of cigarette commercials as well as a number of other adverts. In fact, for more than a decade he put his name to pretty much anything and everything, and why not? It was easy money; the filming or photo-shoots were quick and largely painless, and they kept him in the public's consciousness. The dialogue was often cheesy, but he didn't seem to mind too much, accepting the work for what it was. Advertising Shredded Wheat, this was typical of the dialogue he delivered or was attributed with:

> What a boon is Shredded Wheat for these quick breakfasts snatched before leaving for the studios. I am invariably in a hurry on these occasions, and it fulfils two valuable needs: it is quickly prepared and served, and at the same time it is nourishing and stimulating to an astonishing degree. Because I wanted something that would fulfil these requirements, I found Shredded Wheat. Now it is an essential part of my breakfast, whether I am playing or not. Do by all means use this letter of mine if you wish – I am only too glad to put other people on to a good thing.

Whether advertising Skippy peanut butter or something else, he had adapted to the demands of the day, moved with the times as best he could and would keep busy throughout 1954, during which he made at least fifteen appearances in various TV shows. He also appeared in the Bob Hope and Joan Fontaine vehicle *Casanova's Big Night* that year, expertly playing the comedic villain, Lucio (that avenue hadn't completely dried up!)

The following year was more of the same, TV appearances and commercials, though he would win a small part in the Humphrey

Bogart classic *We're No Angels*, released at Christmas 1955, though it was Bogart, Aldo Rey and Peter Ustinov who were the headliners in a film in which a young Paul Newman also made an uncredited appearance. Taking a healthy $3 million at the box office, it kept Basil's profile visible, if not in the leading roles he'd enjoyed for much of his career.

By the mid-1950s, the Rathbones had moved again, this time to Central Park West to a bigger apartment where Ouida once again had space to entertain and host dinner parties. Their previous residence had been smaller, more modest, and any social gatherings were generally dinner parties for five or six friends. Cynthia was by now a teenager and had grown quite tall, but she showed no signs of wanting to become part of the entertainment industry like her father.

In 1956, Basil bucked the trend of cameo roles and bit parts by being cast in Paramount's *The Court Jester*, playing Lord Ravenhurst, adviser to the king. It was a movie that allowed him to prove he could still play a damned fine villain with all the gusto and energy of man half his age, even if he was actually spoofing many of his earlier action-packed bad guy roles with superb comic timing and delivery. A thoroughly enjoyable romp, the film featured Hollywood star Danny Kaye, who received a Golden Globe nomination for his performance as Hawkins, and at $4 million it was one of the most expensive comedies ever made. A skit on the swashbucklers of the 1930s, it allowed Basil to once again show off his fencing skills, and at 64 he was still as sharp and nimble as ever.

Despite the movie taking just over half its cost at the box office, it has been recognised over the years as something of a classic and Kaye left a huge impression on Rathbone.

He wrote:

There is one other personality-actor-entertainer whose excep-tional talents have always made a deep impression on me whether viewing him 'live' or on the screen or working with him, Danny Kaye. Danny's success does not lie alone in his natural, God-given talents but in a quality that few beginners seem to realize is probably a determining factor in any successful career, WORK! Danny is a prodigious worker, with an aptitude for assimilating and perfecting anything he decides to accomplish. Danny can make one cry just as readily as he can make one laugh: the mark of a truly great comedian. And he has that indefinable quality we call 'class'. In *The Court Jester* we had to fight a duel together with saber. I don't care much for saber, but had had instruction in this weapon during my long association with all manner of swords.

Our instructor was Ralph Faulkner, a very well-known swordsman on the Coast who had specialized in saber. After a couple of weeks of instruction Danny Kaye could completely outfight me! Even granting the difference in our ages, Danny's reflexes were incredibly fast, and nothing had to be shown or explained to him a second time. I was talking to him once about this, and he told me (in effect) that his mind worked like a camera that took perfect pictures, and that he had a very keen sense of mime that could immediately translate the still picture into physical movement. Hear or see anything just once and he could imitate it without the slightest effort. One day, for instance, while 'working out' together, Faulkner introduced us to France's women's foil champion. She spoke little English and that with difficulty and a delicious accent that was adorably feminine. In a matter of minutes Danny was imitating her perfectly, or rather it was not so much an imitation as a perfect facsimile of her manner of speech and her adorable femininity! If such a thing be possible it might be said that Danny spoke his broken French-English better than she did!

Later that year, he filmed *The Black Sheep*, taking a rare lead in a cast that read like a *Who's Who* of horror legends. Playing the unhinged surgeon Sir Joel Cadman, Rathbone lines up alongside Lon Chaney Junior, Bela Lugosi, John Carradine and Tor Johnson. Undoubtedly, at a cost of just $225,000, Bel-Air Productions were able to assemble a stellar cast of actors who had all at some stage been able to command vast fees for relatively small sums, but the picture did reasonably well and was well received.

The *Motion Picture Exhibitor* noted that, 'Rathbone has a grand time as the mad scientist, assisted nobly by some of the best names in the horror field. Audiences should be frightened plenty, and past experience proves that this can mean good grosses … Sure, a lot of it is corny, but it is all good fun in a grisly, frightening manner.'

During the 1950s, Basil continued to appear here and there in various theatre productions, such as *The Winslow Boy*, *One Plus One*, *A Midsummer Night's Dream*, *Hide and Seek* and *Witness for the Prosecution*. He was also on the radio in a number of different ventures throughout the decade, though had Nigel Bruce been around, it's almost certain they would have resumed their lengthy *Sherlock Holmes* radio runs. But that was then, this was now.

His last film of the 1950s was in the fall of 1958, a supporting role in the Spencer Tracey movie *The Last Hurrah*, which, thankfully, it wasn't in terms of his movie career. Though Tracey was nominated for an Oscar, the film lost almost $2 million at the box office.

It was around this time that one of Rodion's three children, Dounia, decided to make an attempt to see her grandfather and so travelled east to meet Basil and Ouida for the first time.

In 2014, Dounia Rathbone – who has since changed her name – recalled the meeting. She said:

> My first and only meeting with him was difficult. I came away pretty sure I didn't want to meet Ouida ever again. She regaled me for two hours with tales of how awful my parents were – and this after over 20 years. I was polite – and furious. Basil was quiet and I came away feeling she had all the power, because he gave it to her. He could be the most brilliant villain on screen, but in his home, it was a different story.

Whatever the issues were in the Rathbone household, it seems that, after thirty years of marriage, they would stay together for better or for worse. They had clearly suffered a number of ups and downs, but perhaps Cynthia has been the glue that had bound them together and as they approached their later years, neither had any intention of leaving the other. In fact, Basil repeatedly said Ouida was his rock and never spoke a bad word about her publicly – it was what others saw that revealed all was not as it had appeared to be.

Basil ended the decade where he had begun – back on the stage. After winning over legendary director Elia Kazan, he won the part of Nickles in *J.B*, taking over from Christopher Plummer from September 1959 until December. The play had already been a huge Broadway success and he later took on the part of Mr Zuss from June 1959 until October 1959. Many felt it again displayed the versatility of Basil as an actor, as he effectively played God and the Devil for each role. It had run for 340 performances and been a monumental success for Rathbone, who enjoyed the experience immensely. The play won the 1959 Pulitzer Prize for Drama and Tony Awards for Best Drama and Best Play, and further enhanced the burgeoning reputation of the 29-year-old Plummer who, like Rathbone, shared a love of Shakespeare having spent time in England performing at the Stratford Festival. Just five years later he would become a huge star thanks to his portrayal of Captain Von Trapp in box office smash *The Sound of Music*.

J.B would tour until the spring of 1960, but worryingly, Basil, by now 68, was taken ill during a performance in Ohio. He recalled:

In January of 1960 in Columbus, Ohio, I awakened one Saturday morning feeling dizzy, and upon rising found I was insecure on my feet. I had retired at a normal hour on the Friday night and had slept well. My condition bothered me, particularly since we had a matinee and evening show at the Hartman Theatre, both of which were sold out with standing room only. I ate a light breakfast and struggled to pull myself together.

As I made-up and put on my costume in my dressing room the dizziness recurred at intervals, and I did something I had never done before. I asked for and drank a triple Scotch whisky, straight! It had absolutely no effect. At the intermission I sent word to our company manager that I would like to see a doctor between shows and get something to help me through the evening performance. As the second act progressed, I became more and more unsteady on my legs and found difficulty in articulating. During the last few minutes of the play I was holding on desperately, my knees were giving way and I was afraid of falling.

After the final curtain call, I walked unsteadily off the stage to be met by two stagehands and our company manager, George Osherin, who literally picked me up and carried me to a waiting ambulance. I protested without effect. All I needed was a doctor and an injection. But my condition had been so apparent out front that Mr Osherin was taking no chances and had asked the fire department for immediate assistance. One aspect of this precipitous but entirely justified action was that the press and the radio got wind of it and fired their reports across the country in such headlines as BASIL RATHBONE COLLAPSES ON STAGE FROM HEART ATTACK – BASIL RATHBONE HAS STROKE DURING PERFORMANCE OF J.B. And this is how my wife and daughter were first informed of my condition! In make-up and costume (somewhat resembling the devil – a black knitted jersey with tight black trousers and a red sash) I was raced to Mount Carmel Catholic Hospital. There, in the emergency room, I was met by Dr Bowers, who examined me thoroughly. I told him I must leave the following night for Milwaukee, where I was due to open on the Monday.

Dr Bowers replied there would be no Milwaukee for me, or anywhere else, for perhaps many weeks. I absorbed the shock and then a few moments later determined to prove him wrong, come what may. I was allowed to phone home to New York and assure Ouida and Cynthia that reports were much exaggerated and that all I needed was a few days' rest. Ouida joined me the following morning after I had had a wonderful night's rest and was feeling fine. It was poor Ouida who looked like the sick one I was supposed to be.

The actual cause of the collapse was never revealed in his autobiography or elsewhere, but a period of convalescence was ordered and, reluctantly, he agreed – but only for a week, before returning to his role in J.B. If there was one thing Basil Rathbone could never be accused of, it was resting on his laurels. He still had much to do.

22

1960–1967

Anything but Elementary

I trust that age doth not wither nor custom stale my infinite variety.

Sherlock Holmes (Sir Arthur Conan Doyle)

The health scare almost certainly made Basil and Ouida reassess their lives, his working schedule, and perhaps even how much time they had left together. Six years older than Basil, Ouida was now 74, so the couple decided to do something that his career had never really allowed time for by embarking on a round-the-world tour. After a short appearance by Basil in *The Winslow Boy* in August, the Rathbones set off on their lengthy vacation.

During the trip, Basil made an appearance at the Princess Theatre in Melbourne, Australia. Whether it was a planned engagement or impromptu invitation is not clear, but it was evidence that in September 1960, their travels had taken them Down Under at that stage. They finished their epic journey in London at Halloween. Whether nostalgia got the better of Basil during their vacation or a desire to end his days at home, he expressed a wish to return to England permanently, though he acknowledged that work commitments in America made that impossible, at least for the immediate future.

Indeed, he had numerous projects lined up including films, TV and radio work, and he was clearly not financially secure. He and Ouida needed financial stability, so there was to be no respite. Despite his incredibly productive career, for thirty-five years he had been the sole breadwinner, save for Ouida's occasional projects here and there. She had played the part of Mrs Rathbone, the doting wife and host, and had she played it extremely well.

Though Basil still had the look of a distinguished English gentleman – which he most certainly was – more and more it was his voice that attracted work. He narrated numerous plays, TV shows, recordings and radio programmes and continued to advertise various products.

The 1961 release of the TV movie *Mystic Stories and Nostradamus* was quickly forgotten, and his portrayal of the villainous Lodac in the 1962 release *The Magic Sword* was fittingly released on 1 April. Basil is one of the few actors to escape with a few crumbs of credit from this cheesy, poorly written fantasy picture aimed chiefly at kids.

Basil continued to take his one-man show on tour around the USA and also visited Central and South America while on the road, playing to medium-sized audiences usually at colleges, universities or women's clubs. He would fly from venue to venue, travelling to Mississippi, Kansas, Maine or wherever there was a willing audience. In an interview in the *Arizona Republic*, he admitted that he did the tour purely for financial needs:

I've had to find some way of making an income other than the hopeless gamble of Broadway. There was a period of 10 years from the closing of *The Heiress*, which was a hit, until I joined the cast of *J.B*, another hit, but I can't afford to wait another 10 years for a Broadway run. Of course, I do pictures here and television there, but it doesn't make a substantial income. Just pocket money.

Many of the names synonymous with Broadway are now doing one-man shows. People such as Judith Anderson, Eva La Gallienne, Charles Laughton and Burgess Meredith. I understand Helen Hayes and Maurice Evans are going out next season. That's a hell of a lot of Broadway stars who are doing this because it's a must. The must is that we have to make a living and most of us simply cannot afford to wait on the theatre.

Half of my programme is devoted to Shakespeare. I feel that in my lifetime, especially lately, the tendency in producing Shakespeare is to try to do something somebody else hasn't done before – not doing what Shakespeare really intended. In particular, I take *Hamlet* and refute, I hope successfully, a great many things that have been imposed on Hamlet, such as he was mad and that he was in love with his mother or that he couldn't make up his mind.

The shows must have made money for Basil, because the production and travel costs alone would have had to have been covered with a decent profit on top – or else, it wouldn't have been sustainable. But was what clear from that interview is that any fortune or savings he had amassed during his heyday were long gone.

As he celebrated his 70th birthday, the movie roles he landed ranged from odd to bizarre, from the cheap and nasty to the downright awful. Here was one of Hollywood's major stars, steadily forced to dismantle his legacy with each bill-paying role he accepted. Had it really gotten so bad that he would take on anything? It seemed so. He signed a two-year deal with independent production company American International Pictures (AIP) in 1962, but it was the studio that was the winner. AIP had a reputation for producing low-budget teen flicks that often had a mix of horror and sex. The studio's formula was to think of a title, produce a graphic poster to promote the film and then attract financiers – only then would the story be created. That Basil Rathbone accepted a deal with AIP spoke volumes of his movie opportunities at that stage.

His first AIP picture was *Tales of Terror*, alongside Vincent Price and Peter Lorre in a trilogy of stories loosely based on Edgar Allan Poe tales. Poe was still popular at the time and Basil and Price's tale – 'Mr Carmichael' – is easily the best of the three. The movie was chalk and cheese to reviewers, who either enjoyed it or found it disagreeable nonsense. Still, the Roger Corman-produced horror flick did decent business at the box office, making $1.5 million and a sizeable profit.

Two more forgettable films followed. *Pontius Pilate* was released in 1962, as was *Two Before Zero* later in the year, but little information of any note still exists on the latter which clearly came and went without much interest. But his next AIP movie bucked the trend somewhat and would arguably be his best for several years. Basil was cast alongside the ageing Boris Karloff, Peter Lorre and the king of camp horror, Vincent Price, in *The Comedy of Terrors*, which did brisk box office business and allowed Basil to not only have plenty of ghoulish fun as John F. Black, but to steal the show in a classic Richard Matheson comedy-horror. Neither Karloff nor Lorre were in great health at that point, and with Basil now 71 it was a miracle the picture had as much energy as it did, though Price was also at his camp horror best in the picture.

The *Los Angeles Herald Examiner* wrote: 'Rathbone is excruciatingly funny in satirizing the Shakespearean actor, who, though ostensibly mortally wounded, keeps rising from the floor to give one more line.'

Scared Silly added: 'Basil Rathbone tears the screen apart as a man who just can't quite seem to stay dead. It is a tour de force performance that also illustrates how underrated a comedy talent Rathbone was.'

Classic Horror joined the chorus of approval: 'Let's give some props to Basil Rathbone for his excellent use of physical humour. I personally never believed he had it in him. His slap-stick role is not how I normally like my Rathbone – I prefer the stern, straight man Rathbone that can be oh-so-mean – but he did a fine, fine job.'

If AIP had designs on following the blueprint of the enormously successful Hammer Film Productions in the UK, *The Comedy of Terrors* came as close as anyone to the look and feel that Hammer had profited so much from. Blood, gore, gothic horror and a script that didn't take itself too seriously, plus a cast of horror legends who may have largely been past their peak (Price apart) but could still ham it up with the best of them.

Yet, though his career in movies was in steep decline and had been for some time, when the Grand Duchess Charlotte of Luxembourg arrived for an official visit to the White House, President John F. Kennedy personally requested that, as part of the events laid on for a special dinner, Basil Rathbone should specifically read 'The Battle of Agincourt' from Shakespeare's *Henry V*. This he did as an encore, and it is hard to imagine a more devoted student to the Great Bard or a better choice to read to European royalty. From budget horror to entertaining JFK – Basil's versatility knew no bounds.

It goes on. Basil kept his hand in TV work – just enough, he indicated at one point, to make sure he wasn't forgotten about, though he never relished the television years of his career, accepting it as a necessary evil. He was a regular guest on the *Merv Griffin Show* between 1963 and 1965, appearing seven times. Griffin later went on to create the popular and long-running American quiz shows *Jeopardy!* and *Wheel of Fortune*.

Sadly, in 1965, he hit rock bottom and it isn't hard to imagine how hard it was for him to stomach the trashy pictures he'd signed up for. Any creative crumbs he'd held on to were gone and this elegant, distinguished and eloquent actor was forced to scrape the barrel. It was purely for the pay cheques, which were becoming harder and harder to find. He filmed his segment of *Voyage to the Prehistoric Planet* in a single day. *Queen of Blood* followed, with Basil earning $3,000 per day in a film where he was professional from start to finish, but the plot, script and set must have felt like he had sold his soul for a dollar.

When his granddaughter Dounia, now in her late 20s, happened to be in Hollywood, she once again reached out to Basil, thinking that she could perhaps see him without Ouida's influence… but was saddened to hear how far her grandfather had fallen. She said:

> I was in Hollywood and, at that time, so was he, so I asked if I could visit him on the set of his latest film. At that time, he was making these 'beach movies' just to make money. His answer was something like … 'This is so awful that I really don't want you to see me doing this.'

I felt sad for him. This is not fact, more conjecture, but I felt that at the end, because Ouida needed to live a certain lifestyle, he was working himself to death, doing lecture tours and B movies that he hated. It's hard to be up so high and fall so far. Especially if he didn't have a supportive marriage.

In an article from *Chiller Magazine*, we perhaps catch a glimpse of the artistic black hole Basil found himself in. It reads:

Before Rathbone finished his last day of shooting *Queen of Blood*, he was asked to film more scenes to be edited into another Soviet science fiction film *Planet of Storms*, also owned by Roger Corman. The plot involved the first spaceship in the year 2020 to reach Venus whose only communication with the Earth is with a space vehicle which circles the planet in orbit. The astronauts face many unexpected dangers including prehistoric monsters. Rathbone performed the same duties, wore the same costume, and worked on the same set as he did in *Queen of Blood*. But this time his name was Professor Hartman. The film was never released theatrically, however, did surface on television as part of a syndicated package in various parts of the country. Both films were directed by Curtis Harrington.

Harrington recalled the film:

We were all in awe of Rathbone – a star who worked in some of the biggest pictures form the Golden Age of Hollywood – now working on a low budget non-union film for $3000 a day. Because some of our sets weren't ready, we fell behind on our short shooting schedule, so the actor had to work an extra day. We found out later he went to the Screen Actors Guild complaining he wasn't paid his overtime! But he was a great guy to work with anyway.

Despite his dislike of TV, it was ironic that it was this medium more than any other that introduced Basil Rathbone and Nigel Bruce to a whole new audience and gave Basil something of a cult following among the American youth. The *Sherlock Holmes Theatre* allowed Basil to host a run of Holmes films on TV for the first time and the movies proved popular and ran for more than a year, with Basil introducing his own pictures at the beginning. In some ways, his movie career had come full circle.

Yet it seems without doubt that times were hard, financially.

In September 1965, filming began on *The Ghost in the Invisible Bikini*. Once again, it was an AIP movie and therefore skimped and scraped wherever possible. Roger Corman was, for some, a more successful Edward D. Wood of his day. Cast alongside Boris Karloff for the last time, the daughters of Frank Sinatra and Dean Martin also had leading roles in what was AIP's seventh beach party flick. It was also the last. The film was a box office flop.

As ever, Rathbone and Karloff's class showed through, ensuring their reputations as Hollywood legends – albeit from a different era – remained intact. The *Los Angeles Times* patronisingly claimed: 'Old timers give the picture some class.' While *Scared Silly* wrote: 'Basil Rathbone excels here as the slimy Ripper.'

It was a B-movie and Basil did his best, as he always had. It was just way beneath him, even if he had the good manners to pretend it wasn't.

In Basil's 75th year, he filmed the bizarre Mexican movie *Autopsy of a Ghost* alongside John Carradine. Shot in Mexico City, the picture was a disaster, though Rathbone and Carradine at least made the most of the filming. Carradine said:

> Basil was hopping and jumping and leaping around like a man of 30. But at the end of the day he was tired – because of the altitude, a mile high there [in Mexico City]. At dinner one night he said, 'John, I'll never do this again.' And I said, 'What do you mean?' And he said, 'Work at this altitude.' Within a few months, he was gone.

It was a terrible picture and was never released in the States. But sadly, there was a worse one to follow. *Hillbillys in a Haunted House* starred John Carradine, Basil Rathbone and Lon Chaney Junior and was an absolute turkey of a film from start to finish. Yet this cheap, amateurish film would prove to be Basil's epitaph – his last screen role, which is a minor tragedy in itself.

Ouida had now turned 80 and their daughter Cynthia was approaching 30 and working for an agency in New York, but there would be no further films for one of England's greatest actors. On 21 July 1967, while at home in New York, Basil suffered a heart attack and died. He was 75.

The *New York Times* reported:

> The tall, impeccably mannered actor, who was 75 years old, was found dead on the floor of his study at his home on 135 Central Park West by his daughter Cynthia. She said her father had suffered a heart seizure several years ago but had been in good health recently. A funeral service will be held at 11am Tuesday in St James' Episcopal Church as Madison Avenue.

Close to 400 people attended Basil's funeral, during which actress and close family friend Cornelia Otis Skinner read Elizabeth Barrett Browning's 'How do I love thee?' – a favourite of Basil's – and also Robert Brooke's 'The Soldier':

> If I should die, think only this of me:
> That there's some corner of a foreign field
> That is for ever England.
> There shall be, in that rich earth a richer dust concealed;
> A dust whom England bore, shaped, made aware,
> Gave, once, her flowers to love, her ways to roam,
> A body of England's, breathing English air.

Shortly after his passing, Calvin T. Beck, renowned editor of the horror magazine *Castle of Frankenstein*, wrote:

> Especially saddening is the knowledge that, typical of itself, Hollywood, indeed the whole entertainment industry so stupidly

underestimated him and, by so doing, remaining blind to the tremendous impact that he had all over the world. (Quite unnecessary to mention his most recent years when he was aging, no longer in demand, and how AIP 'rediscovered' him at bargain basement rates for its rapidly growing little film empire.)

BUT ... those of us, who sat through his films over and over again ... we knew! So did those millions who select just a handful of stars and dub them Immortal. Indeed, so did the staid, usually stuffy, but internationally respected New York Times:

They paid their final respects with a glorious tribute in their July 22, 1967 edition by not placing the article in the back, where, normally, all obituaries go, but in a position reserved solely for great dignitaries, kings and presidents: On page one ... in a long, glowing two-columned article!

During the several days Basil Rathbone lay in state, until he was removed for burial from St. James' Episcopal Church on Tuesday, July 25, 1967, thousands of people came to view him and pay their last respects – at times, the lines stretched all the way outside the funeral chapel, down the street and around the corner – on the final day, because of the hour of the funeral (10:00 a.m.), attendance dwindled down to several hundred.

If there is a theology mantling the divine art of drama and film-making, then Basil Rathbone deserves sanctification. For having lost a beloved Leader, a part of us has been interred within his hallowed coffin.

Oh, what a lonesomer, hapless world it shall be without him.

Indeed, it was. An elementary observation, if ever there was one.

Epilogue

Following his death, Basil's estate was valued at just $12,000, which was divided between Ouida and his son Rodion, and Ouida received $2,600 from Basil's life policy.

He was buried at the final resting place of such screen legends as Joan Crawford and Judy Garland. Fitting company for one of Hollywood's finest and most talented actors.

Interestingly, Basil had been slated to appear in *The Blood Beast Terror* later that year. Rathbone was signed to play the part of Dr Mallinger (a mad scientist), but he died before filming began. The role of the doctor went to Robert Flemyng.

Satanic Pandemonium reviewed the movie, and mulled over what might have been as they wrote:

> Probably the biggest disappointment of all is that Dr Mallinger was supposed to be played by the late, great Basil Rathbone, but after his death, the role went to Flemyng. Thanks to the latter's performance in one of my favourite films, Freda's *The Horrible Dr Hichcock*, I will never say anything bad about him, but ... Rathbone.

Peter Cushing played Inspector Quennell in *The Blood Beast Terror*. If Basil Rathbone had lived to make that film, it would have been the only time those two great actors worked together – one approaching the peak of his career, the other at the end of his distinguished journey. *The Blood Beast Terror* was filmed on location in London and would have undoubtedly given Basil a lot of pleasure. Conversely, just as he had been revered in America in the 1930s and 1940s and perhaps frostily received in England for a while, the reverse was now true, and while the American movie industry had turned its back on him, studios such as Hammer would have welcomed him with open arms. Had he returned a decade earlier, at his villainous best, he would have almost certainly been involved in picture after picture from Britain's prolific box-office hitmaker.

Moreover, Cushing, a confirmed Holmes enthusiast who possessed a large collection of Conan Doyle's original stories in *The Strand* magazine, had perhaps come as close as anyone to portraying Sherlock Holmes as well as Rathbone with his role in Hammer's 1959 production of *The Hound of the Baskervilles*. To have had the best ever Sherlock Holmes actor and arguably the second best in the same picture would have been a treat for all Holmes fans.

The truth was, as his granddaughter Dounia observed, Basil Rathbone deserved better – much better. He deserved to have been able to have a dignified retirement and perhaps take the odd part that came along on stage or in film. With his prolific working life and the number of huge box office successes he'd enjoyed, he should have been able to enjoy his later years and bask in the glory of years gone by. He should have been able to come home to England, something he seemed to desperately want to do but couldn't afford to, and instead was forced to accept roles in movies that were, to be frank, an insult to his reputation. They put food on the table and nothing else. It was an incredibly sad end for a quite brilliant actor and, even some eighty years or so on, it is safe to say that nobody played Sherlock Holmes like Basil Rathbone. Almost certainly, nobody ever will.

Perhaps Leonard Maltin, writing in *Film Fan Monthly*, best summed up Basil Rathbone's career when he wrote: 'Some actors, while excellent performers, fit into a mould and, when they are gone, other younger actors fill their shoes. Other actors, however, are unique and in a sense, irreplaceable. One of these people was Basil Rathbone.'

Few would argue with those sentiments.

Sadly, within a decade, Basil's wife and daughter were dead, too. On 4 June 1969, Barbara Cynthia Rathbone died aged just 30, just two years after Basil's death. She passed away at the Roosevelt Hospital with the *New York Times* listing the cause of death as 'acute anaemia'. A former colleague from Hockaday Advertising Agency, where she had worked for several years, believed Cynthia's death was ultimately caused by drink and drug issues, but that was never conclusively proved. She had lived in Upper Manhattan at 15 West and 72nd Street with her mother.

Five years later, on 29 November 1974, the irrepressible Ouida Rathbone also died, aged 88, also at Roosevelt Hospital, and was reportedly destitute and alone at the time of her death. Her funeral was held at the same church where Basil's had been held and she was interred next to her husband and daughter at Ferncliff Cemetery in Hartsdale, New York. In a little over seven years, father, mother and daughter had all passed away. And less than two years after that, on 8 September 1976, Marion Foreman, Basil's first wife, also died. She passed away at Denville Hall in Northwood, London, at a retirement home for actors, aged 89.

Dounia Rathbone recalled an affectionate memory of Marion, revealing:

> Marion cut quite a figure. She was women's liberation long before the words were coined. She lived with us in Chicago for a year or so while I was studying ballet and Caroline was running 'show trains' with a prominent producer. When we went out, she always wore that Shakespearean cape, long and suitably dramatic. We were about to cross a busy street and we all cautioned her to take care for traffic. Her response was to walk out into the middle of traffic, dramatically swirling her cape, saying in her magnificent British accent… 'THEY WOULDN'T DARE!'

It was the end of an era.

Basil's son Rodion died in 1996 and is survived by three children, Heloise, Rodion and Dounia.

Heloise's daughter – Basil's great-granddaughter – also Dounia, was 11 when her father Rodion passed away. She recalled:

> I like Basil's movies as well. My mom and I have watched many. We had audio records of a lot of his Sherlock Holmes shows and I would listen to them quite often. We have a DVD of him as Scrooge in the Christmas movie, which was a rare find and basically my entire family got a copy.
>
> My mom would always say, 'He is a brilliant actor, but not a brilliant father.' My grandfather (Rodion) didn't know a lot about Basil either since he walked out on Babu (what we call my grandfather) when he was young. There is actually a movie about war that Basil starred in that my grandfather was in also, by Basil's request I believe. Basil played a commanding officer and my grandfather played a pilot (which he was in real life). In the script, Basil is supposed to send Babu on a suicide mission, but he made them change the script because he didn't want to send his son to die. So, in the movie, a different character gives the order. I found that pretty interesting. I think he felt guilty for leaving Babu as a child.
>
> I don't recall my grandfather talking about Basil much, if ever. I think it was too hurtful for him. I can't really remember if we talked about Basil what Babu's reaction was. Babu died when I was 11 and had Alzheimer's the final years of his life.
>
> I was told Basil's wife spent all his money on parties and nonsense, so Basil died broke. As for my mother, Heloise, she still remembers Basil since meeting him was a very important experience for her. She only met him for about 5 minutes after one of his plays on Broadway. He told her to wait for him to get changed out of costume and everything, but he never came back to her.

Though the family's recollections of Basil Rathbone clearly contain a lot of hurt, it is perhaps the knowledge that they were never able to meet him and get to know him properly that rankles more than anything else. They are unanimous that Ouida was the barrier and that he wasn't strong enough to overrule her. It is a pity he never got to know his grandchildren better, as he had shown many times with children in his professional life and personal life that he was a doting, caring father-figure. Maybe he knew that if he did get too close to Rodion's children it would inevitably end in tears, with Ouida's powerful personality and will to erase the life he had before he met her evident on many occasions. It is something we will never truly know.

What we do know is Basil Rathbone's portrayal of Sherlock Holmes remains the benchmark that others aspire to reach and so few rarely achieve. Cinema and television's most played character, with more than 250 different productions, each actor that takes on the role of Sir Arthur Conan Doyle's greatest creation will be inevitably compared to Rathbone. None have bettered him.

Jeremy Brett is widely considered to be the closest, with the English actor playing Holmes on TV for a decade before his untimely death aged 61. Arguments rage to this day as to whether Brett or Rathbone should be considered the greatest of them all. But it is a fact that, even to this day, Rathbone's Holmes movies remain hugely popular and are rarely off television.

For most fans of the Great Detective, if they are asked to close their eyes and imagine Sherlock Holmes, it's not Benedict Cumberbatch, Robert Downey Jr or Jeremy Brett they see; it is a black-and-white image of Basil Rathbone, snooping around on the foggy back streets of London or skulking around the Great Grimpen Mire.

Yes, he grew to hate the role – but ultimately, in later years, he made his peace with Holmes. Had he known that his and Nigel Bruce's movies would be as popular today as they were eighty years ago, he might even have grown to like him again.

Index

You may also enjoy …

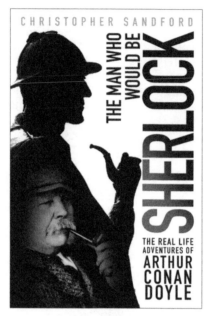

978 0 7509 6592 7

Using freshly available evidence and
eyewitness testimony, Christopher
Sandford draws out the connections
between Conan Doyle's literary output
and factual criminality, a pattern that
will enthral and surprise the legions
of Sherlock Holmes fans. In a sense,
Conan Doyle wanted to be Sherlock
– to be a man who could bring order
and justice to a terrible world.

The destination for history
www.thehistorypress.co.uk